Party & Society

Political Sociology series

Daniel Béland, *What is Social Policy?*
Understanding the Welfare State

Cedric de Leon, *Party & Society*

Nina Eliasoph, *The Politics of Volunteering*

Hank Johnston, *States & Social Movements*

Richard Lachmann, *States and Power*

Siniša Malešević, *Nation-States and Nationalisms*

Andrew J. Perrin, *American Democracy*

Party & Society

Reconstructing a Sociology of Democratic Party Politics

Cedric de Leon

polity

First published in 2014 by Polity Press

Polity Press
65 Bridge Street
Cambridge CB2 1UR, UK

Polity Press
350 Main Street
Malden, MA 02148, USA

ISBN-13: 978-0-7456-5368-6
ISBN-13: 978-0-7456-5369-3(pb)

A catalogue record for this book is available from the British Library.

Typeset in 11 on 13 pt Sabon by
Servis Filmsetting Ltd, Stockport, Cheshire
Printed and bound in Great Britain by TJ International Ltd, Padstow, Cornwall

For further information on Polity, visit our website: www.politybooks.com

For Emily, Ellis, and Attie

Contents

Introduction

The orienting objects of inquiry in contemporary political sociology are the state and civil society. The prevailing definition of the state is Max Weber's notion of an actor or institution that "claims the *monopoly of the legitimate use of physical force* within a given territory" (Weber 1946: 78; emphasis in original). The state is distinguished, therefore, by its military sovereignty, although it is also widely acknowledged to be the principal steward of social services (e.g., unemployment insurance, old age pensions) and infrastructure (e.g., roads and bridges). The accepted definition of civil society is the space between the state and the market, which includes interest groups, social movements, religious organizations, and other voluntary groups (Cohen and Arato 1992; Habermas 1991). Of the latter, social movements loom largest in the political sociological imagination.

Political parties are distinct from these other entities because of their control of the system of nominations, elections, and appointments to political office (e.g., president, secretary of defense, city councilperson). They preside, in other words, over the formal institutional machinery that many of us associate with the democratic process. Further, political parties that prevail at the polls assume the reins of state power. This phenomenon of "party government" means that politicians direct the foreign and domestic policy of their respective communities. Accordingly, political parties have been key players in the most significant and painful social transformations of our times. The rise and fall of the Bush administration and the Blair government, for instance, are important for understanding not only American and British politics, but also the War on Terror and the recent recession, the knock-on effects of which continue to impact the lives of millions of people around the world. Parties are also implicated in the troubled advent of electoral competition in Iraq, Afghanistan, and the former Soviet bloc, as well as the rise of Islamism and socialism in the Middle East and Latin America respectively.

Despite the centrality of political parties in democratic life and their influence on current affairs, the formal parties literature is paradoxically ill-equipped to grasp the complexity and dynamism of their subject. In practice, parties stand in a fluid continuum with the state and civil society, such that it is sometimes difficult to discern where one of these three entities begins and another ends. For example, the Muslim Brotherhood, which rose to power in Egypt after the Arab Spring democratic revolution, is a political party and social movement at once that found itself exercising formal state power. Yet the scholarship on political parties tends to proceed as if little to no such fluidity exists. In voter-centered approaches, which supply the dominant[1] theories in the field, the state is almost entirely absent, and the remaining relationship between party and society is lopsided, with voters inexplicably bearing most of the responsibility for running democratic party politics, and parties playing a passive role. Parties are implicitly defined as remote organizations that reflect the social divisions, familial loyalties, or policy preferences of a given community. Party-centered approaches, which are older and less prominent than their voter-centered counterparts, are more open to the fluidity described above. Party, state, and society interact and sometimes fuse on these accounts, but in ways not fully applicable to the contemporary political scene. Here parties are implicitly defined as organizations that are to varying degrees autonomous from their constituents and thus pursue their own motives and objectives.

Given the current state of the art, this book makes three broad contributions. First and foremost, it attempts to re-establish the place of parties alongside the two orienting objects of inquiry within political sociology. Second, it reveals the disconnect between the actual dynamism of political parties on the one hand and academic approaches to political parties on the other. Third, it suggests that sociology offers possible ways out of this impasse. While sociologists are as guilty as others for popularizing a static view of political parties, they also furnish an array of conceptual tools that are uncommon in the other disciplines of the field. Sociologists tend to be more skeptical than political scientists, economists, and psychologists, for example, of the notion that voters and politicians are rational, utility-maximizing individuals. They are more likely to suggest that meaning, culture, symbolism, history, and institutions shape the texture and outcomes of democratic party politics. There are important exceptions of course, and the ground is noticeably shifting as other social sciences go through their own cultural and historical turns, but on the whole, there is a stronger impulse in sociology to investigate the importance of such factors because of its theoretical lineage.

To arrive at such conclusions, I have had to teach myself (for the purposes of peer review) the vast literature that appears in this book. Part of my vision, therefore, is to write the reference manual I never had. It is by no means an exhaustive work, nor is it the first of its kind, but it is to my knowledge the only one that foregrounds sociology's classical and contemporary contributions to this area of inquiry. In doing so, the book aims to broaden, and thereby enrich, our sense of the scholarly terrain.

This is not just another handbook, however, for implicit in the inclusion of sociology are several inter-related arguments about the scholarship on democratic party politics. First, the book suggests that to truly understand the field, one must be able to follow the ongoing cross-disciplinary debate among political scientists, social psychologists, economists, *and* sociologists. Specifically, the frequent truncation and caricature of the so-called "sociological approach" as an artifact of the mid-twentieth-century Columbia University sociology department impoverishes our knowledge of where we have been and impairs our instincts for where we can go next.

This is related to my second point, which is (as the subtitle of this book suggests) to recuperate, and cultivate an appreciation for, the diversity of sociological perspectives on this subject. Just as there is no one approach to democratic party politics in political science, so, too, is there no one approach in sociology. It is, of course, true that sociologists inaugurated the first modern voter studies, but they were founders, and are contemporary practitioners of, the three party-centered approaches in the second half of this book as well.

At the same time, I do not wish to resume what Converse (2006) recently called an embarrassing "turf war" between the disciplines. Thus, my third argument is that while it is important to acknowledge the healthy diversity of theoretical and methodological tendencies in the social sciences, a purely jurisdictional battle would obscure more than it illuminates. For example, as I have noted above, the dominant approaches in the field, including one that is sociological in pedigree, share something in common: they are voter-centered, meaning that they focus on the individual voter as the primary unit of analysis (see, for example, Carmines and Huckfeldt 1996). Voter-centered analysts, like pollsters, rely on survey research, assuming that the answers of individual respondents supply the most accurate explanation for why a voter chooses a certain party or candidate. These individual vote choices are then assumed to add up to an explanation for short-term electoral outcomes (e.g., the winner of a single election) and long-term trends or alignments (e.g., the dominance of a single party for a generation). This is known as "methodological individualism," and it is pervasive throughout the social sciences. In this context, a challenge to the "scientific rigor" of an academic other is likely to circle back on itself.

My fourth claim has to do with insularity, for the debates among voter-centered approaches in part I of this book are largely isolated from those of the party-centered approaches in part II. Thus, the concept of the "partisan voter" (chapter 2), whose behavior stems from familial loyalty to a political group, emerged in reaction to the concept of the "social voter" (chapter 1), whose behavior is shaped by loyalty to a social group such as one's class or religion. With a few notable exceptions, the lines of debate among party-centered approaches are almost as self-referential and correspond roughly to the dispute between "conflict" and "order" perspectives in the social sciences. For instance, the "oligarchical party" (chapter 4) is a conflict perspective, because it assumes that the organizational demands of mass suffrage (i.e., where most people have the right to vote) make it inevitable, paradoxically, that political parties will dominate their constituents. The order perspective, represented here in the chapter on "the functional party" (chapter 5), concedes the point that there is a political elite, but insists that such an elite is beneficial to democratic society.

My fifth argument is about a different sort of boundary, namely the "hard" or "non-porous" boundary that scholars imagine separates political parties from all other entities. This is less true of classical party-centered theorists like Weber, Michels, Lenin, and Gramsci, but on the whole party scholars tend to be agnostic, for instance, on "party movements" (e.g., Green and indigenous parties) and what I call "omnibus parties," organizations like Hamas, Hezbollah, and the African National Congress that exhibit features of parties, states, and social movements simultaneously. Contemporary research on these topics is generally confined to social movement theory and other areas beyond, or at the margins of, the formal parties literature.

To address these problems, the book remaps the field by including the diversity of sociological approaches beyond the Columbia model. In doing so, it recuperates important clues for how we might grasp the intersection of party, state, and society and thereby come to terms with the richness and complexity of current democratic politics in practice.

The First Debates

The aforementioned divide between voter- and party-centered approaches may be traced back to the first debates over political parties. For many of us, a system of legal opposition is simply part and parcel of life in a free society. In fact, however, legal mass parties – not just informal camps of political elites in a legislature, but formal organizations that mobilize dissent in the electorate – are a relatively recent phenomenon, dating to the early-nineteenth-century United States (see, for example, Duverger [1951] 1963: xxiii; Sartori 1976: 13, 19–22).

The American experience begins with the British.[2] Prior to remaking themselves into "Americans," political elites like John Adams, Thomas Jefferson, and James Madison were Englishmen who understood themselves to be free men. This requires some explanation, as the folklore about the American Revolution suggests that the colonists were merely "British subjects" and therefore subservient in every way to the arbitrary misrule of King George III. This is not quite the case. If Adams and his associates were galled by the practices of the king, it is because the "Whig" or "Country" tradition of British politics, which inspired successive revolts against the royal "Court," had made them believe that they were entitled to certain liberties even if the king reserved to himself the role of head of state or "sovereign." This ideology or world-view is often referred to as "republicanism," according to which men[3] in affairs of state were expected to act in the interest of society as a whole, rather than their own narrow interests. Within this framework, a "party" was a group of men who conspired to take hold of the state in pursuit of a private agenda. As such, parties carried the stigma of being disloyal to the Crown (in Britain) or the Republic (in America).

There were broadly speaking three streams of opinion about political parties in mid-eighteenth-century Britain – antiparty, qualified antiparty, and pro-party – but the pro-party stance was far and away the least popular. This minority view is exemplified by the work of Edmund Burke. In *Thoughts on the Cause of the Present Discontents* (1770), Burke wrote, "Party is a body of men united for promoting by their joint endeavours the national interest upon some particular principle in which they are all agreed" (Robbins 1958: 510; White 2006: 6). By defining party as a champion of "national" interest, Burke deliberately sought to refute the widely held assumption that organized opposition was intrinsically selfish and therefore hostile to society as a whole. Although he acknowledged that some might use political parties for their own predatory interests, he insisted, "when bad men combine, the good must associate." Organized opposition prevented society from degenerating into unprincipled factional strife and thus was "necessary for the full performance of public duty" (Hofstadter 1969: 32; Sartori 1976: 9).

More pervasive than Burke's pro-party position were antiparty views, which ranged unevenly from the outright denunciation of parties to more measured claims that parties were inevitable but must be controlled. Toward the denunciation end of the spectrum was Lord Bolingbroke, who, like most commentators of the mid-eighteenth century, viewed parties in general as vehicles for the pursuit of private interest. In the *Idea of a Patriot King* ([1749] 1965), he wrote that parties are "numbers of men associated together for certain purposes and certain interests, which are not, or are not allowed to be, those of the community by others." Because they sought to subvert the good of society for selfish reasons, organized opposition to the government was, for Bolingbroke, "treasonable in tendency." The lone exception to this rule obtained when the world was turned upside down. That is, when the government itself conspired to subordinate society to the royal Court, then there was nothing more patriotic than a party that organized to stop the government in its tracks. Such a party, however, would be temporary and therefore not really a party at all: it would install a likeminded "Patriot King" (who was protective of society) and then promptly dissolve itself. "A party thus constituted," he hedged, "is improperly called party. It is the nation speaking and acting in the discourse and conduct of particular men" (Hofstadter 1969: 21, 23; Sartori 1976: 6–7; Wilson 1988: 424).

Others like David Hume (and later James Madison) resigned themselves to the notion that parties were an unfortunate reality in politics and therefore worked to mitigate their most destructive tendencies with constitutional checks and balances. In "Of the coalition of parties" ([1758] 1854), Hume wrote, "to abolish all distinctions of party may not be practicable, perhaps not desirable, in a free government." But to prevent partisanship from escalating into revolution or civil war, it was necessary to steer aspects of public policy over which Parliament had control away from contentious questions like religion to questions, say, of economy in which moderation was supposedly more likely. Moderation, Hume wrote, "is of advantage," whereas "overactive zeal in friends is apt to beget a like spirit in antagonists" (Hofstadter 1969: 26–7; Sartori 1976: 8).

What is common to all three approaches to party and society is an attempt to justify and manage dissent in such a way as to avoid the appearance of treason, on the one hand, and to prevent differences of opinion from evolving into unprincipled opposition, or worse still, civil war and revolution, on the other. This was a tricky needle to thread, but it was even trickier in the American context.

The United States was peculiar in a world of monarchs as the first state with "divided sovereignty," wherein official power did not reside with the king or queen but was instead shared by way of compact between the people and their government. This unprecedented state of affairs combined with the inherited anti-partyism of British tradition introduced a contradiction in the heart of the American political system. The constitution furnished political elites with resources over which to compete (voters) and allowed the people to sustain or remove their representatives through popular elections. However, antipartyism stigmatized any form of organized opposition as disloyalty to the Republic; when any coherent dissent emerged, the state threatened violence and imprisonment.

Thus, in his presidential *Farewell Address*, George Washington denied the right of either political elites or the mass of voters to associate in opposition to government policy. "The very idea of the power and the right of the people to establish government," he insisted, "presupposes the duty of every individual to *obey* the established government" (emphasis added). For Washington, organized opposition contradicted this duty: "All obstructions to the execution of the laws, all combinations and associations, under whatever plausible characters, with the real design to direct, control, counteract, or awe the regular deliberation and action of the constituted authorities, are destructive of this fundamental principle and of fatal tendency" (Washington [1796] 1904: 217–18).

Accordingly, early American political elites depended on coercion to silence dissent. For example, in 1794 when farmers in Pennsylvania, Virginia, and Kentucky rebelled against a tax on whiskey, George Washington raised an army roughly the size of the entire revolutionary militia to crush them, though the insurrection ended before government soldiers arrived on the scene. Later in 1798, as the United States contemplated joining Britain in a war against France, Washington's allies in Congress, called "Federalists," maneuvered to break the "Republican" opposition led by Thomas Jefferson, who argued that the United States should take the side of France, a fellow revolutionary republic. In response, the Federalists raised a standing army and passed the Alien and Sedition Laws. Three alien laws subjected immigrants (a majority of whom were thought to be Jefferson sympathizers) to longer naturalization periods, deportation, and imprisonment, while the Sedition Law further restricted the use of libelous words against the government (Ferling 2004: 110–11; Wilentz 2005: 62–4).

The rapid succession of such national crises prompted a few leading Republicans to justify political parties as a barrier to the kind of selfish factionalism that had brought American society repeatedly to the brink of civil war. This group's pre-eminent theoretician was Martin Van Buren, who claimed that a hidden "aristocracy" was seeking either to remake the United States in Britain's image or to bring the Republic down by sowing dissension from within. Revising Bolingbroke's idea of the prerogative of the Country to form a party in the face of a royal conspiracy, Van Buren argued that foiling aristocratic plots would require a *permanent* disciplinary device – the Democratic Party – that could unmask otherwise unidentifiable traitors. This party would serve to "excite a salutary vigilance over our public functionaries" and "tear the masks from several, who without having been exposed . . . might have been able . . . to have passed for what they are not." Van Buren's rationale therefore dropped Bolingbroke's original call for a temporary organization, while retaining the notion of the party as the embodiment of the people's will and thereby casting all other parties as illegitimate. Indeed, Van Buren's justification for the Democratic Party was that it "was to be a party of the whole sovereign democracy," as opposed to "selfinterested minorities" (Hofstadter 1969: 16, 18–24, 252; Leonard 2002: 9, 11, 17; Van Buren 1973: 512; Wilson 1988: 433).

From there, a new generation of politicians could practice partisanship in ways that the post-revolutionary electorate and political elite understood and accepted. On the one hand, they used antiparty themes that expressed impatience with disloyalty and unprincipled opposition: none of the early parties framed itself as the vanguard of a special interest group, but of American society as a whole. On the other hand, the early parties employed rhetoric and practices that drew heavily on the wartime imagery of the revolution, positioning themselves as the institutional counterweight to the hidden remnants of British treachery, espionage, and aristocracy. Thus, whereas the political party had once been seen as a conspiracy to disorganize society, by 1840 the new practice of partisanship transformed the party into the guardian of the Republic (de Leon 2010).

The early American experience has numerous implications for us as we prepare to engage the rest of the book. Before a system of legal opposition took hold, the state counteracted dissent with the threat of violence. This is not to suggest that political parties have not since used violence to advance their agendas (the German Nazi Party is a classic counterexample), but rather that political parties have since become a widely accepted and useful (though by no means a universal or sure-fire) way to organize dissent *peacefully* (see, for example, Key [1942] 1964: 203–5). This is a core claim of the functional approach, which views parties as essential to a stable democracy. Moreover, parties in contemporary democracies and authoritarian regimes alike claim to represent the national will instead of narrow "selfinterested minorities," in much the same way that the Democratic Party did in Van Buren's time. The rhetorical claim persists despite the fact that parties rarely if ever truly represent all the constituencies of society. This ironic fact of democratic life is an important touchstone of the oligarchical approach, which is quick to mock the disingenuousness of parties claiming to speak on behalf of everyone.

Next, the early American case serves as a poignant reminder as we evaluate theories that presuppose the legitimacy of political parties. The positive valuation of legal opposition was not then, nor is it now, necessarily self-evident. Even for America's founding generation, who today are often eulogized as paragons of civic virtue, political opposition was a high stakes gamble that could very quickly escalate into civil war and invite violent state repression. Political opposition continues to be a dangerous business. Until very recently, all opposition parties in Egypt were officially banned, while in Turkey the courts shut down parties regularly, including the predecessors of the now governing AKP. This is to say nothing of Singapore, China, Vietnam, Cuba, North Korea, and Syria, which are all one-party states. In Russia, where liberal democracy allegedly took hold after the collapse of the Soviet Union, Vladimir Putin's ruling "United Russia" party tolerates little to no dissent. Organized opposition to globalization has prompted state violence in modern democracies such as the United States, Canada, South Korea, Argentina, and Italy. The contentious story of early American party formation is therefore not as distant from us as it seems.

Organization of the Book

For the purposes of this book, however, the most important implication of these first debates is that they turned on one key question, namely, whether or not parties were a help or hindrance to free society. The book is organized primarily by the level of analysis of competing approaches (the individual voter in part I, the party in part II), but the divergent levels of analysis overlap with another distinction: the extent to which each approach re-engages the central question of the first debates.

With the possible exception of V.O. Key's (1966) later work in *The Responsible Electorate*, the voter-centered approaches in part I of this book sidestep this question. The debate among these approaches centers on a different problem: which variable is the most important determinant of vote choice? Chapter 1, "The Social Voter," features what most social scientists will recognize as the so-called "sociological approach." It suggests that social "cleavages" such as class, racial, and religious differences shape the decisions of individual voters. The approach consists not only in the early Columbia studies, but also in two restatements: those of Knoke (1976) and Manza and Brooks (1999). Chapter 2, "The Partisan Voter," features the "social psychological" or Michigan model, which holds that the best predictor of vote choice is the political allegiance of one's family. The approach begins with the foundational works of Campbell, Gurin, Miller, Stokes, and Converse, and concludes with their contemporary proponents. Chapter 3, "The Issue Voter," consists of three theoretical traditions – spatial theory, issue voting, and realignment theory – all of which argue that vote choice is anchored in the rational policy preferences of voters.

In contrast, the first two chapters in part II recuperate the question of whether parties are a help or hindrance to free society. "The Oligarchical Party" approach (chapter 4) holds that parties are fundamentally anti-democratic. It features three traditions, beginning with the Iron Rule of Oligarchy, continuing with what some view as its descendant, power elite theory, and ending with the patronage tradition and its critics. "The Functional Party" approach (chapter 5) contends that parties are essential to democracy. It consists of four lineages: functional parties, responsible parties, elite but functional parties, and pluralism. I also devote a separate section in this chapter to Seymour Martin Lipset, for his vision of parties not only bridges the other lineages in chapter 5, but is also one of the few that engages in debate with voter-centered approaches. Chapter 6, "The Exclusive Party," may be read as a way out of the debate between the two preceding approaches, in the sense that it elides the question of whether parties promote democracy to focus on how parties differentiate their own leaders, operatives, and constituents from those of their adversaries as a matter of practice. It starts with the literature on legislative coalitions, including Riker (1962), Aldrich (1995), and

Poole and Rosenthal (1997); continues with a theoretical interlude on the political construction of groups and interests; and ends with the Marxist tradition. In chapter 7, I marshal evidence from the preceding chapters to summarize my main claims and conclude with directions for future research on the intersection of party, state, and society.

Choices and Limitations

As we prepare to move on to the first substantive chapter of the book, let me offer a few caveats in the event that the reader expects something that is not forthcoming. Because my goal here is to sketch out the broad outlines of debate, I will not be evaluating the field from the vantage point of the exclusive party approach with which my own work is associated. My emphasis instead will be on drawing out, as faithfully as I can, the theoretical implications and assumptions – the big ideas – of each piece, tradition, and approach. Accordingly, my attention to empirics will be limited to key findings, and methodological innovation will receive only passing mention when necessary to illustrate the theoretical payoff. I should emphasize, if it is not clear already, that each aforementioned "approach" is not itself a single coherent theoretical tradition, but a set of traditions that share a similar vision of the relationship between party and society. Nevertheless, the reader's progress will make reasonably good sense I hope: when I cover a "tradition," I start with its earliest modern statement (i.e., without returning to the Enlightenment or the Ancients), and end with a more recent and notable synthesis.

Anyone who is aware of the world of ideas outside the United States and Europe will no doubt recoil from the book's ethnocentrism. I am guilty as charged. There is undoubtedly a wealth of scholarship on parties written in languages I do not read well, especially from Latin America, where scholars engage regularly with their English-speaking counterparts to the North. To compensate for this important oversight, I have tried my best, where appropriate, to explain concepts by using international or generic examples. The problem, of course, is that as good scholars, many of the authors in this book are careful to say that their findings only apply to the American or European context. Where that is the case, I will be equally careful not to misrepresent their ideas as applicable to other settings. Occasionally, I will make an effort to point out that such ideas beg for comparative research.

Acknowledgments

I include my acknowledgments unconventionally in the introduction to this book, because writing a critical review of a literature as vast as this one is necessarily a biographical exercise. My vision of the intellectual terrain reflects to some degree my training as a graduate student in two areas of sociology – political and comparative historical sociology – that are concerned with certain programmatic questions, among them the contested origins of democratic transitions, revolutions, and state formation. It may also be helpful to know that I began graduate school in the 1990s, in the wake of the "historical" and "cultural" turns in sociology, when the foregoing questions were being analyzed as the effects of historical conjunctures, contingencies, and discourses.

To those who are familiar with such trends, it will make sense that I did my graduate work at the University of Michigan. My dissertation committee consisted of Howard Kimeldorf (my chair), Julia Adams, George Steinmetz, and Mayer Zald of the sociology department, and Mills Thornton, a political historian of the American South. Though this book is not a revised version of my dissertation, it nevertheless bears the mark of my teachers (I hope not to their everlasting dismay). I discovered my interest in party politics in Mayer Zald's class on cultural sociology. My preoccupation with American politics grew out of Mills' seminar on antebellum political history. I acquired my appreciation for theoretical lineages in a class co-taught by Julia Adams and George Steinmetz. And I learned the craft of sociological research and exposition from my chair, Howard Kimeldorf. Howard and Julia have remained important mentors to me since leaving Michigan, and I owe much of my success thus far to them.

Equally important to my socialization as a scholar, teacher, and political observer are my peers. In Ann Arbor, my closest friends and intellectual sounding boards were Andy Clarno, Claire Decoteau, Mark Dilley, Chandan Gowda, Karen Hébert, Elise Herrala, Bashar Tarabieh, Mark Villacorta, and Anna Zogas. In Providence, I have been blessed with bright students and wonderful friends and colleagues, especially my junior faculty comrades-in-arms and my mentors, Eric Hirsch, Neil Riordan, and Julia Jordan-Zachery. My closest allies outside the professoriate have been Deus Cielo, Kyle Quadros, Michael Rodriguez, and Louis Rothschild. For helping to shape my particular view of party politics, I would like to thank my longtime collaborators, Manali Desai and Cihan Tuğal. Those in the wider profession who have been supportive of me in the cause of "bringing parties back in" to sociology include Tony Chen, Lis Clemens, Barry Eidlin, Julian Go, Jeff Haydu, Rob Jansen, Isaac Martin, Ann Orloff, Kent Redding, Dylan Riley, Eduardo Bonilla-Silva, Dan Slater, and Lynette Spillman.

This book would not have been possible without the patience and generosity of readers, reviewers, and editors. Joe Cammarano and Adam Slez read the entire first draft of this manuscript. Jeff Pugh met with me to discuss omnibus parties. Emma Longstaff was my first contact at Polity Press, and Jonathan Skerrett has since shepherded this project to fruition. Polity's anonymous reviewers, in addition to casting a gratifying vote of confidence in my favor, recommended changes that vastly improved the overall architecture of the book and the second draft of the manuscript.

Finally, it is a commonplace to thank one's family for a reason. This book has required too much sacrifice from those who share my life on a daily basis. My wife, Emily Heaphy, is an academic, too, and has given generously of her time and energy. I dedicate this book to her, our son, Ellis, and our saintly companion, Attie.

Part I

———

Voter-Centered Approaches

1

The Social Voter

In this chapter, we begin with the first modern voter studies, which were conducted by sociologists at Columbia University in the 1940s and 1950s. The key finding of this research was that social "cleavages" or divisions like class and ethnicity were the decisive factors shaping individual vote choice. The chapter continues with a brief word on two challenges to the social voter approach, one by a former Columbia graduate student, Seymour Martin Lipset, and another, which held that social class was declining as a significant predictor of vote choice relative to cultural values. The chapter ends with two restatements of the social voter approach and an epilogue on the class vs. culture debate.

The Columbia Model

Imagine for a moment that you are walking down the bread aisle of your local supermarket. The brand names catch your eye, and as they do, your mind associates to vaguely remembered advertising campaigns, some of which fit, and others of which don't fit, your taste in, say, politics and lifestyle. After being buffeted back and forth between the competing brands – this one commercial, that one local, this one white bread, another multigrain – you arrive at the end of the aisle and turn around to make your choice.

The process and determinants of consumer choice comprised the original interest of Columbia sociologist Paul Lazarsfeld.

Peter Rossi (a classmate of Lipset) wrote that the impetus for the early voting studies at Columbia was two-fold. Early in his career while still in his native Austria, Lazarsfeld had been interested in the "psychology of choice," beginning with occupational choice and eventually arriving at consumer choice. Later, as director of Columbia's Office of Radio Research, which would become the famous Bureau of Applied Social Research, he turned his attention to the effects of propaganda and advertising. Having been unable to secure sufficient funding for these earlier projects, however, he proposed another study, funded by the Rockefeller Foundation, on the determinants of *vote* choice in the 1940 U.S. presidential election between the Democratic incumbent, Franklin Roosevelt, and the Republican challenger, Wendell Willkie (Lipset 1996: 3; Rossi 1959: 15–16).

Lazarsfeld hypothesized that the process of arriving at vote choice would essentially mirror that of consumer choice. As a voter made her way through the election season, she would be subjected to the presidential campaigns, which would, in turn, interact repeatedly with her own predispositions, until at last she made her decision. Accordingly, Lazarsfeld and his colleagues at the Bureau designed a "panel study" that could capture the effects of the campaign as the individual voter "walked down the aisle" toward the election. A sample of voters from Erie County, Pennsylvania, was interviewed a total of seven times during the course of the campaign.

As it turns out, the results of the study provided embarrassingly little support for the original hypothesis. They found, first, that the overwhelming majority of voters did not change their minds from the first interview (when they identified their preferred candidate) to the last. Evidently, the campaign had minimal effect. Only 54 out of a sample of 600 respondents reported switching their votes. Second, the "background questions," asked routinely at the beginning of many surveys to establish the respondent's basic biographical information, turned out to have the highest correlation with vote choice. For example, "Of all rich Protestant farmers almost 75% voted Republican, whereas 90% of the Catholic laborers living in [the city of] Sandusky voted Democratic"

([1944] 1948: 26). From this, Lazarsfeld and his team constructed an "index of political predisposition" consisting of three variables: socioeconomic status, religion, and rural vs. urban residence, which they held accounted for most of the variation in vote choice. Perhaps the most famous sentence from that study, published in 1944 under the title, *The People's Choice*, became the calling card of the emerging "sociological approach" to political behavior: "a person thinks, politically, as he is, socially. Social characteristics determine political preference" ([1944] 1948: 27).

Having found that campaigns had minimal impact on vote choice, the Bureau resolved to do a follow-up study, this time under the leadership of Bernard Berelson and in a sample of voters from Elmira, New York, during the 1948 U.S. presidential election season. Their goal was to uncover the reasons that social characteristics had been so decisive in explaining political differences. That panel study, which was published in 1954 under the title, *Voting*, was cut down to four interviews; its questions were changed to capture the social dynamics of home and community life. Their data suggested that class, ethnic, and residential divisions continued to provide "the most durable social bases for political cleavage." Thus, they found that those who identified with the middle and upper classes voted more Republican than those who identified with the lower or working classes. With respect to ethnicity, they discovered that "White native-born Protestants vote Republican more than minority ethnic groups" (1954: 75).

The *reason* that class, ethnicity, and residence were so decisive, however, was not that they triggered a reflex in the voter's psyche that automatically connected social group loyalty to party. This is an unnecessary caricature of the sociological approach (see, for example, Przeworski and Sprague 1986: 7–8). Rather, social characteristics matter because they correspond to concrete social relationships in voters' communities.

Berelson et al. argue that three mechanisms translate social characteristics into political differences. Political disagreement in a community originates, first, with the mechanism of "social differentiation." This is based on the simple assumption that government policies impact different groups in different ways. Take the example of income disparity. A graduated income tax system does not affect the rich and poor in the same way. The rich are expected to contribute more as a percentage of their income than blue-collar workers, because they can afford to do so. Workers, in contrast, do not pay the same percentage as the rich do, because such a percentage would hit their smaller paychecks harder. Moreover, because workers are often one paycheck or illness away from financial disaster, they benefit disproportion-ately from the social safety net, which most people contribute to, but which is sustained in large part by the contributions of the wealthy. The rich and the poor therefore tend to vote for different parties, or so the argument goes. But if social differences are strong enough to *spark* political differences, they are not by themselves able to *maintain* those differences over time. Family, friends, and colleagues must "transmit" political predispositions from one generation to the next. Finally, and in a related vein, the political predispositions of a large social group remain intact when there is minimal internal disagreement. To maintain consensus, there must be regular physical and social "contact" among people who are already politically inclined in the same direction (Berelson et al. 1954: 74). The punchline, then, is that because the conditions of political division – social differentiation, transmission, and contact – are met most effectively in class (e.g., workplace), ethnic (e.g., church), and residential (e.g., neighborhood) settings, they offer the most plausible explanation for why some people vote for one party, and others vote for a different party.

Exit Lipset

Though the Bureau's work was avant-garde for the time, it was quickly eclipsed by other approaches. One of these was advanced by a former Columbia graduate student, Seymour Martin Lipset. Lipset will receive more detailed treatment in chapter 5 (see pp. 116–22), but he requires a brief word here, as students of parties view him exclusively as an adherent of the Columbia model.

Lipset's differences with the psychology of vote choice had been germinating as early as 1943, when he wrote a little known class paper for his dissertation advisor, Robert K. Merton (Lipset 1988). That paper became *Union Democracy* (Lipset et al. 1956), a book that, along with *Political Man* (Lipset 1960) and *Party Systems and Voter Alignments* (Lipset and Rokkan 1967), used the survey method to shift attention away from the determinants of vote choice towards the conditions that favored stable democracies. By far the most vital condition was "conflict within consensus," and the most important institution that achieved this condition was a competitive party system (Buxton 1985: 223). The function of political parties, he held, was to provide an avenue through which the conflicts between a community's primary social groups could be expressed but contained, such that electoral defeat could be tolerated and the authority of the state could remain legitimate (Lipset 1960: 1–4). In this sense, Lipset's project is primarily a *party-centered* explanation for social order, and only secondarily an individualistic analysis of vote choice.

His 1967 work with Stein Rokkan, which is sometimes seen as an extension of the Columbia model, must be read in this light. Typically (and I have been as guilty of this as anyone), scholars portray Lipset and Rokkan as working out the founding social cleavages (e.g., church vs. state, elite vs. non-elite) of European party politics. There is some logical support for this reading. For them, parties do not generate social cleavages; cleavages emerge as a result of national and industrial revolutions, sometimes well before parties appear on the scene. That social cleavages shape voter allegiances is clear in their account. But for Lipset, social conflict does not a stable democracy make: by itself conflict is liable to undermine democracy and give way to totalitarianism of one stripe or another. A necessary ingredient – indeed, the *sine qua non* of Lipset's vision – is the stabilizing influence of political parties. In my reading of him, then, Lipset is not the sequel to the Columbia model (as we shall see, Knoke and Manza and Brooks deserve that distinction more), so much as he is the most illustrious, and perhaps the only, bridge-builder between the voter- and party-centered approaches that have divided the field in two.

The Decline of Class Voting and the Rise of the Values Voter

Lipset and his associates were not the only ones who distanced themselves from the Columbia model. Others argued that class was not nearly as important to vote choice as sociologists had believed. The anti-class thesis turned on two claims that were often, though not always, linked: first, that class voting was in decline, and second, that the class cleavage was being supplanted by a new cleavage, namely, cultural values. Culture is a catch-all word in political parlance for non-economic concerns such as environmental degradation, abortion, crime, homosexuality, and opposition to the welfare state (often framed as "personal responsibility").

The ascendancy of Margaret Thatcher in the 1970s spurred arguments about the declining significance of class in Great Britain. Though Donald Stokes is a founding figure in the partisan voter approach, his work with David Butler ([1969] 1974) in *Political Change in Britain* is widely seen as providing support for the Columbia model's emphasis on class (specifically parents' class and respondent's occupation) as a powerful predictor of vote choice. The reactions to Butler and Stokes ranged from outright rejection of their original conclusions to more nuanced claims. For the former camp, McAllister and Rose (1986) wrote, "The old class-equals-party model of politics is no more – if it ever was" (p. 1). Franklin (1985), by contrast, sought a middle ground. Butler and Stokes, he said, were right about the election of 1964, but the basis of electoral choice in Britain had since changed (Franklin 1985: 5). Franklin went on to explain that changes in social structure were at least partly responsible for undermining class voting. Economic growth, which created a more affluent, home-buying working class, and government policies, which mitigated class segregation in schools, conspired to make class antagonism less salient for British voters (Franklin 1985: 57, 60, 67).

Back in the United States, Ronald Reagan's victory in 1980 occasioned fresh post-mortems of the New Deal welfare state and of the salience of class in American politics. Fraser and Gerstle's

(1989) edited volume, *The Rise and Fall of the New Deal Order*, is typical of this genre. The editors begin their book with the ominous claim that "When Ronald Reagan assumed office in January of 1981, an epoch in the nation's political history came to an end. The New Deal, as a dominant order of ideas, public policies, and political alliances, died" (1989: ix). What was that order and what brought it down? Jonathan Rieder's (1989) essay in that volume, "The Rise of the 'Silent Majority,'" provides the most direct answer. Rieder explains that white working- and middle-class Americans were initially drawn to the economic or class-based liberalism of the New Deal Democratic Party, which acknowledged the importance of taming class inequality after the trauma of the Great Depression. At the same time, these less affluent white voters were religiously conservative and threatened by the gains of the Civil Rights Movement. Additionally, they tended to favor a muscular posture in the Cold War with the Soviet Union. It was these traditionalist Democrats – values-voters – who balked at their party's latter-day support for civil rights and opposition to the war in Vietnam.

Ron Inglehart's (1990) book, *Culture Shift*, followed quickly on the heels of Fraser and Gerstle. Inglehart's international values survey data provided the empirical support for the culture thesis in much of the western industrialized world. Inglehart's narrative begins with the claim that the welfare state blunted the cruelest dislocations (e.g., unemployment, homelessness, infant mortality) of free market capitalism. Having thus solved the basic problems of physical and economic security, the welfare state enabled voters, especially working-class voters, to turn to "post-materialist" preoccupations like environmental degradation. Thus, he writes that "a gradual shift ... toward greater emphasis on belonging, self-expression and the quality of life" is due to:

> the unprecedented levels of economic and physical security that have generally prevailed in these countries since World War II, and to the emergence of the welfare state ... the publics of advanced industrial society are increasingly likely to take this kind of security for granted – and to accord a high priority to self-expression both in their work and in political life. (1990: 11)

Though the work of Ben Wattenberg (1995) more closely resembles a neo-conservative manifesto than a scholarly assessment of late American politics, it is nevertheless considered an important exemplar of the genre. Drawing on a series of public opinion polls, Wattenberg suggests that American voters since at least the 1980s had become more concerned with crime, welfare, and so-called "racial preferences" than they were with the economic or class-based issues that sustained the Democratic Party's dominance during the New Deal. The values-oriented rhetoric of both Ronald Reagan and Bill Clinton are thus taken to be the winning formula in American politics: "I suggest here that whichever political party, whichever political candidate . . . is seen as best understanding and dealing with that values issue – will be honored . . . at the polls in 1996 and, I bet, for a long time after that" (1995: 10–11).

The Social Voter Strikes Back

It was in the context of the foregoing critiques that the two major restatements of the sociological approach emerged. These latter-day arguments might be called "neo-classical" in the sense that they returned to the original preoccupations of Lazarsfeld and Berelson. Back was Berelson's original attempt at a multi-level explanation for why social characteristics mattered in engendering political differences in a community. Ethnicity and residence also made a comeback to round out the caricatures of the sociological approach as having been obsessed exclusively with class. Back, too, was the emphasis on individual vote choice, though this new generation of sociologists would draw on national- instead of community-level survey data.

The first restatement was David Knoke's (1976) *Change and Continuity in American Politics*. In that piece, Knoke conceded that class differences "play a relatively minor role in structuring political party affiliations in postwar America," accounting for no more than 5 percent of the variation among voters (1976: 89). Nevertheless, Knoke insisted that religion, race, and residence remained important factors in voting behavior (1976: 36, 58, 109).

26

For example, with Lazarsfeld and Berelson, he confirmed that Protestants were still significantly more likely to vote Republican than Jews and Catholics were (1976: 36). With respect to race, region, and residence, Knoke found that over time, "Democratic affiliations among southern whites plummeted while Independent affiliations doubled" (1976: 58). Finally, the theory Knoke supplied for the persistence of social cleavages recuperated Berelson's original emphasis on the importance of "contact" within social groups. He argued that political parties are diffuse "secondary" groups with whom voters have very little contact; it is only through the "penetration" of political sentiment in non-political primary (family) and secondary social groups (e.g., unions) that party loyalties can become and remain viable (1976: 11).

The second restatement of the social voter thesis was Manza and Brooks' (1999) *Social Cleavages and Political Change*. Like Knoke, they found that religion, race, and region remain important cleavages in American politics, but added that gender and class are also decisive. Whereas American women once tended to divide evenly between the two parties, in the late-twentieth century they voted increasingly Democratic. Further, Manza and Brooks pushed back against rumors of the decline in class voting. They insisted that the latter were based on the crude binary, used in most polls and surveys, of manual versus non-manual workers. To capture current class effects on voting, they suggested, one must update measures of class to reflect the more fine-grained class structure of post-industrial America. Specifically, they found that liberal professionals have left the Republican Party and become the second largest Democratic constituency, unskilled workers have moved to the center, and the self-employed have become more Republican (1999: 5).

Their theoretical framework aims to account for not only long-term shifts in voter loyalties (i.e., realignments), but also short-term shifts (e.g., the defeat of an incumbent). This is important, because social characteristics such as ethnicity and gender tend to be stable: if a Muslim votes for one party in 2012 but votes for another party in 2016, it is difficult to show that her Islamic identity was responsible for the shift, since she was Muslim all along. To account for this and other difficulties, Manza and Brooks took another stab at Berelson's original attempt to explain the link between social characteristics and political differences.

The authors contend that cleavages must operate at three levels for them to have significant effects on both vote choice and the character of the parties' electoral coalitions.[1] The first level at which a cleavage must operate is objective structural position (e.g., a voter's race, gender, or class), because cleavage has an "'empirical' component rooted in social structure." But one's objective position is not enough to become a matter of political significance. An Ethiopian Jewish woman who is a recent immigrant may vote on the basis of her treatment as a black person in the American context, as a woman, as a Jew, as an immigrant, or any combination of these identities. So the second level, "group identification and conflict" suggests that "social groups making up a cleavage field" must "adopt conflicting forms of consciousness." To return to the previous example, for our Ethiopian Jewish friend to choose a party based on her immigrant identity, it is critical that social groups, say, native-born and foreign-born citizens, hold divergent attitudes towards immigration. But that is *still* not enough to make a bona fide cleavage. Manza and Brooks explain that in their third-level, objective structural position and conflicting consciousness must be "expressed" through "individual interactions, institutions, and organizations, such as political parties, which develop as part of the cleavage" (1999: 33–5). If the conflict over immigration does not manifest itself in personal conflict or, for example, in competing social movements, then it is unlikely to manifest itself as a factor affecting individual or group voting. In that case, cleavages that do have some organizational basis will be more salient. Our voter could cast her ballot based on her Jewish identity, because the local Jewish Community Center hosted a town hall meeting on Iran's nuclear ambitions. If, on the other hand, pro- and anti-immigrant rights groups have done sufficient lobbying and put their concerns on the radar of the political parties, then it becomes at least more likely that our voter will make her choice based on her immigrant status.

As such, Manza and Brooks offer any number of ways to

account for short- and long-term shifts in voting behavior. A long-term predisposition of, say, white men to vote for the Republican Party is unlikely to change unless an alternative cleavage, say, class, makes itself felt at all three levels. If it does, then it may do so for a short or a long time. If an economic recession is sufficiently deep, then an unemployed white male worker, who comes into conflict with his more affluent neighbors, may shift his partisan loyalties permanently, provided that the major parties take similarly contrasting positions. However, if the worker loses his job in October and regains it in December, then the vote he cast for the new party in November may not get his vote again.

The Class vs. Values Debate Rejoined

The class vs. values dispute re-emerged with the publication of Thomas Frank's *What's the Matter with Kansas?* in 2004. The book was an attempt to explain why white working-class voters supposedly acted against their economic interest by voting for the Republican George W. Bush in 2000. Frank argued that this demographic was seduced by the so-called "culture wars," which caused internal class division over abortion and the teaching of evolution (i.e., instead of creationism) in public schools. The book was pilloried in academic circles, not least in political science (see, for example, Fiorina 2005). Rather than end on a low note, however, I will conclude with a synthetic attempt, on the part of Brewer and Stonecash (2007), to moderate the debate that followed.

For them, the dispute was cast in terms too stark to be useful. In answer to the question of which cleavage – class or culture – dominates American politics, they answer, "class concerns and cultural issues both matter." In this, it is important to point out that neither cleavage overshadows the other. With respect to class, voters are concerned primarily with the growing inequality of opportunity in areas such as "education, health care, housing, and overall quality of life." With respect to cultural concerns, they find that "the conflict is driven by different ideas of what constitutes appropriate behavior, different views on right and wrong." Accordingly, they argue, both the class and cultural cleavages operate more or less simultaneously and at equal strength (2007: xv).

*

To conclude, we return, as we will do in each successive chapter, to the central arguments of the book. First, I argue that to understand theories of democratic party politics, one must understand the place of sociology among them. In this chapter, we see that the modern voter studies began with sociologists at Columbia University. Later approaches to vote choice must therefore be understood at least in part as a reaction to Lazarsfeld and his team. Second, I want to insist that sociological perspectives are diverse even within the same approach, and cannot be reduced to the early voter studies. The work of Lipset, Knoke, and Manza and Brooks provide persuasive evidence on this point. The charge of "social determinism" is a plausible reading of *The People's Choice*, but it is not true of anything that comes afterwards. Beginning with *Voting*, sociologists have attempted to explain in ever more complex ways how one's social group shapes (but does not determine) individual vote choice. Third, I contend that a disciplinary turf war would obscure the similarities among the competing approaches to democratic party politics. We will not know for sure until the end of the third chapter, but already we see that the Columbia studies and their descendants pose the individual as the primary unit of analysis. That is, the scholars in this chapter are most interested in why an individual votes as s/he does. It is also too early to tell how insular the voter- and party-centered scholarly communities are (my fourth argument), but Lipset's distinction as perhaps the only theorist of party to bridge this divide foreshadows the developmental arc of the field. Finally, I want to argue that because scholars tend to view parties as entities, separate from the state and civil society, they often undertheorize the ways in which the three intersect with each other. The social voter approach is largely preoccupied with civil society in the very limited sense that voters' ties to the institutionalized forms of class and ethnicity (e.g., unions, churches) are the central determinants of vote choice. By comparison, the approach is relatively silent on the state, and with the possible exception of Manza and Brooks, parties are viewed as both remote and passive, the recipients of voters' group loyalties.

2

The Partisan Voter

In the years following the emergence of the social voter approach, a group of social psychologists (Angus Campbell and Gerald Gurin) and political scientists (Warren Miller, Donald Stokes, and Philip Converse) at the University of Michigan inaugurated a competing theoretical tradition, the so-called social psychological or Michigan model. The canonical work in this literature is Campbell et al.'s (1960), *The American Voter*. Briefly, by way of preview, the latter held that social cleavages such as class, ethnicity, and residence do not correlate well with individual vote choice. A superior explanatory variable, which they gleaned from *national* survey data (to repeat, Columbia's were *community* studies) was party identification, or just "party ID." The variable is something of a misnomer in that it has little to do with parties per se; it is a political identity transmitted over the generations through one's family. That is, rather than loyalty to social group, the Michigan model privileged inherited loyalty to *political* group, a loyalty anchored in emotional attachments to one's parents' or grandparents' partisan commitments.

But just as "the social voter" came under fire from those who doubted the salience of social group loyalties (see pp. 24–6), so, too, did the partisan voter endure scrutiny from those who would insist that people were not the uncritical partisans that Michigan social scientists made them out to be. Three literatures emerged as a result. One group (e.g., Miller and Shanks 1996; Smith 1989) offered a straightforward defense of the Michigan model, especially the continuing importance of party ID. Another group engaged in a related back-and-forth over the extent to which the American electorate was polarized (e.g., Baldassarri and Gelman 2008; DiMaggio et al. 1996; Green et al. 2002). Still another group, whose work I categorize under "schema theory" below, offered to be more specific about the processes that make symbolic, as opposed to rational, thinking important for understanding how people cast their ballots and form impressions of candidates and parties. For this reason, I refer to the various bodies of work in this chapter as exemplars of "the partisan voter" approach. The genesis, defense, and elaboration of the approach are recounted below.

The Case for Loyalty to Political Group

If the Columbia model privileged loyalty to one's social group as the decisive factor shaping vote choice (see pp. 19–22), then the first reaction from political science was to insist that loyalty to one's *political* group was more important. This intervention was no party-centered alternative to sociology's voter-centered model, however. On the contrary, political scientists expanded on Lazarsfeld's original vision by administering surveys to nationwide, instead of community-level, samples of American voters. Moreover, the variable they advanced as a competitor to social cleavage was "party ID," which gestured to the activities of party organizations or leaders only in passing. The far more critical source of an individual's party ID was her or his affective attachment to the partisan loyalties of the family.

Though the first study in this style was published in 1954, it was Key and Munger's 1959 essay that made the first programmatic statement on the importance of political allegiance. Key and Munger began with one of the more crisp and famous lines in the history of anti-Columbia critiques: "The style set in the Erie County study of voting, *The People's Choice*," they wrote, "threatens to take the politics out of the study of electoral behavior" (1959: 281). By this, they mean that Lazarsfeld's method is

33

unable to account for either long-term partisan attachments or short-term fluctuations in voting behavior. To make their case, they examine county-level electoral returns in the state of Indiana from 1868 to 1900. Key and Munger first point out that because Lazarsfeld et al. only take a snapshot of individual decisions in a single election cycle (the 1940 U.S. presidential election), they miss the stability of partisan attachments over time. The stability of Democratic Party counties in Indiana from 1868 to 1900, for example, suggests that "there tends to be a standing decision by the community" in matters of politics (1959: 286). This "standing decision" is not a rational calculation, but rather a partisan loyalty that endures despite changes in interest and the disappearance of issues that initially created partisan patterns. Partisan attachments endure not only across time, however, but also across space, for counties with different social characteristics (e.g., rural vs. urban counties) may vote for the same party, and conversely, counties with the same social characteristics may vote for competing parties. "The long persistence of county patterns of party affiliation," therefore, "points toward a 'political' grouping at least to some extent independent of other social groupings" (1959: 287).

Additionally, Key and Munger suggest that the sociological approach cannot explain why a given social determinant may be important at one point in time, and unimportant in the next. For example, religious background was an important determinant of voting in the 1928 U.S. presidential election: protestant counties voted Republican, whereas Catholic counties voted Democratic. The problem is that religion was much less important in the 1924 and 1932 elections. Presumably, if religion were truly a decisive factor in vote choice, and if voters' religious affiliations do not change from one election to the next, then religion should show up as a persistent determinant of voting behavior, but it does not. A more plausible explanation is once again "politics," for it was in 1928 that Al Smith, the first-ever Catholic candidate for the U.S. presidency, secured the Democratic nomination (1959: 292).

The Social Psychological or Michigan Model

By way of introduction to the first book in the Michigan tradition, I should say a word about V.O. Key as some eyebrows may be raised by his inclusion in this chapter. Key was a paradoxical figure in the partisan voter approach. He was an early supporter of the Michigan project and indeed pushed to have it funded as the chair of the Political Behavior Committee of the Social Science Research Council (Converse 2006: 605). However, as we shall see in the next chapter, he would later criticize the Michigan model in his book, *The Responsible Electorate* (1966). Be that is it may, Professor Key introduced Campbell, Gurin, and Miller's 1954 book, *The Voter Decides*, by proclaiming, "In this volume we have the most impressive analysis yet made of a national election by the survey method." Auto enthusiasts will appreciate that he compared the Campbell study to Gallup's 1936 national survey "as the new Cadillac does to the first Model T" (Key 1954: ix–x).

Campbell et al. begin with an implicit homage to Columbia's early voter-centered studies. In contrast to "aggregate data, such as election statistics," which are reported on a precinct and county basis after the vote, they point out, "The methodology of the sample survey makes it possible to reach and obtain information from great masses of people on an individual basis." The authors also used an abbreviated panel study in that they collected responses before and after the election to see if factors relating to the pre-election context affected the actual vote (1954: 1–3).

But that is as far as they went in support of the Columbia model. They demonstrate, for example, that the shift from the Democratic to the Republican parties between 1948 and 1952 took place in *all* social groups, thus limiting the explanatory or predictive power of social groups on vote choice. Indeed, on their account, Lazarsfeld's "index of political predisposition" (see p. 21) yielded a prediction of the 1948 election not much better than chance (1954: 85). The Michigan alternative was to measure the effect of "intervening variables" on vote choice, "the psychological variables which intervene between the external events of the voter's world and his ultimate behavior" (1954: 85–6). Of the six variables they tested,

three had the biggest effect on vote choice: party ID, issue orientation, and candidate orientation. Thus, they wrote, "those people
who felt themselves strongly identified with one of the major
parties, held strongly partisan views on issues which were consistent with those of their party, and were strongly attracted by the
personal attributes of their party's candidate expressed preference
in nearly every case for the candidate their party put forward"
(1954: 182–3). Though issue orientation would later drop out of
the social psychological model, we have nevertheless in the 1954
piece the variable with which Michigan would forever become
associated: party ID.

The canonical work of the Michigan social psychological tradition is not this first book, but the 1960 follow-up: *The American
Voter* (or *TAV*). It was here that Campbell, this time accompanied
by Converse, Miller, and Stokes, annunciated their last word on
the sociological approach (thereafter the Michigan school would
turn to the front opened up by the concept of the issue voter).
Their critique of Lazarsfeld and Berelson was two-pronged,
though noticeably more conciliatory than that which appeared in
1954. The first, as always, was that social characteristics, being
generally stable from election to election, could not explain short-
term fluctuations in voting behavior, where, for example, someone
who identifies strongly as a Democrat nevertheless votes for a
Republican in a given election (Campbell et al. 1960: 17). The
reason now put forward for sociology's shortcoming, however,
was not that the index of political predisposition was entirely
wrongheaded, having a predictive power no better than chance.
Social characteristics mattered to be sure, they conceded, but they
were *distant* causes of vote choice, whose effects could not be felt
among the more powerful "proximate" causes that were observ-
ably decisive. This alternative approach may be summed up in
their metaphor of the "funnel of causality." This metaphor, which
originated in a term paper Converse wrote as a graduate student,
was his attempt to "halve the distance in the dispute" between
Columbia and Michigan – a discussion he said he found "embarrassing" at the time (Converse 2006: 606). Thus, while giving an
inch, the Michigan team continued to insist that only the proximal

or immediate psychological factors, which are *politically* relevant and closest to the vote in time, explain most of the variation in voting behavior (Campbell et al. 1960: 24–5, 34–6). These immediate "objects of political attitude" in the 1952 and 1956 U.S. presidential elections were "the personal attributes of [the candidates]; the groups involved in politics and the questions of group interest affecting them; the issues of domestic policy; the issues of foreign policy; and the comparative record of the two parties in managing the affairs of government" (Campbell et al. 1960: 67).

Having thus disposed of the Columbia model's inability to account for short-term fluctuations, they then turned to long-term factors that explained the stability of individuals' voting behavior over time. In this, they held that such stability was not anchored in social characteristics, but a stable *political* characteristic: party ID. Party ID is not defined by formal membership in the party, or active participation in the party apparatus, or even by voting record since, as we have seen, people with contradictory voting records may self-identify as "Strongly Democratic or Strong Republican." Rather, they write, "Generally this tie is a psychological identification," which is a "sense of attachment with one party or the other," adding, "We use the concept here to characterize the individual's affective orientation to an important group-object in his environment," namely "the political party" (Campbell et al. 1960: 121–2). Note, however, that party ID is not primarily about the activities of political organizations or leaders, but about voters' *feelings* about the party, which are traceable to one's upbringing. They write, "an orientation towards political affairs typically begins before the individual attains voting age ... this orientation strongly reflects his immediate social milieu, in particular his family." They continue, "The high degree of correspondence between the partisan preference of our respondents with that which they report for their parents may be taken as a rough measure of the extent to which partisanship is passed from one generation to the next." In short, "party identification has its origins in the early family years" (Campbell et al. 1960: 146–8).

The American voter was therefore *not* the clear-eyed, deliberative, and informed voter attributed to classical theories of democracy; on the social psychological account, s/he was an uncritical partisan. This point was further elaborated in three classic essays, one by Donald Stokes, and two by Philip Converse. The Stokes article (1963) was perhaps the first clear signal that the Michigan school had turned its attention away from Columbia and moved on to confront rational choice theory, represented most famously in political science by Anthony Downs' 1957 book, *An Economic Theory of Democracy* (see pp. 59–61). Without going into great detail (as we will spend half of the next chapter on Downs and his descendants), that book advanced what is now known as "spatial theory."

Spatial theory turns on several assumptions as to how people arrive at their vote. Downs imagines a range of issue preferences arrayed on an ideological scale of 0 to 100 where 0 is the far left (e.g., anarchism) and 100 is the far right (e.g., fascism). Voters are said to have "peaked" preferences along that scale, such that, for example, a moderately liberal voter might have a preference of 35 against the war in Iraq (e.g., "I wish the U.S. had never invaded, but now that they're there, they should leave responsibly"), and a left-wing pacifist who is against war under any circumstances might have a preference of 10. Competing parties likewise pitch their preferences along that scale (logically where a plurality of voters cluster), and voters then pick the party or candidate who is closest to their position. The theory is "spatial," because the voter's decision is based on the *proximity* of the party to her issue preferences, and that decision is fundamentally a rational one, because the voter knows where s/he and the party stand on the issue and is thus able to *calculate* proximity.

Stokes directed his fire primarily at two assumptions. The first is "unidimensionality," the assumption of "a single dimension of political conflict," organized on an ideological spectrum of left to right. One problem with this assumption, he argues, is that political conflict is *multidimensional* in character. For example, voters tend to have different attitudes toward welfare policy and foreign policy, and those attitudes have absolutely no relation to each other. Moreover, the Michigan data suggest that voters do not think in terms of an ideological scale of left to right or liberal to conservative. Indeed, they are hardly able to articulate what these distinctions mean, let alone correctly identify which party is liberal, and which is conservative. He writes, "When our respondents are asked directly to describe the parties in terms of the liberal-conservative distinction, nearly half confess that the terms are unfamiliar. And the bizarre meanings given the terms by many of those who do attempt to use them suggest that we are eliciting artificial answers that have little to do with the public's everyday perceptions of the parties" (1963: 370).

The second of spatial theory's problematic assumptions is "ordered dimensions," the notion that there is "one ordered set of alternatives of government action that the parties may advocate and the voters prefer." The alternatives range from completely against government action to completely in favor. Here Stokes makes the famous distinction between "position-issues" and "valence-issues." Downs has in mind position-issues, which are "those that involve advocacy of government actions from a set of alternatives over which a distribution of voter preferences is defined." For example, on the issue of government intervention in the economy, voters can choose among a set of alternatives from no intervention at all to robust intervention. What spatial theory leaves out are the "valence-issues" that dominate the typical election. Valence-issues are "those that merely involve the linking of the parties with some condition that is positively or negatively valued by the electorate." This involves "credit or blame" for a condition that is presently upon us (e.g., an existing or recent recession) *or* a guess of "who is more likely to" manage the matter if we are talking about an impending condition (e.g., the rise of a new world power). No party is for or against valence-issues, and voters do not choose between parties, one of whom is, say, for prosperity, and the other for financial distress. Instead, voters make their choices based on a "diffuse" or general sense – rather than a rational choice – that a given party has or has not presided over a period of prosperity (1963: 372–3).

Accordingly, Stokes recommends that Downs and his associates adopt "scope conditions" on the applicability of spatial theory. He concedes that spatial theory may be useful in moments of "strong ideological focus" (e.g., the New Deal, Civil War), when elections really are about one political conflict and the issues are position-issues. Spatial theory is less useful for moments of weak ideological focus, which comprise the norm in electoral politics (1963: 376).

Stokes' critique dovetails nicely with Philip Converse's essays of the mid-1960s. Converse's 1964 piece, "The Nature of Belief Systems in Mass Publics," turns on two interrelated concepts. A "belief system" is a "configuration of ideas and attitudes in which the elements are bound together by some form of constraint or functional interdependence." "Constraint" denotes coherence or consistency across a range of issues (1964: 207–8). The key point to take away is that for a voter to say that she is "conservative," for example, it is not enough for her to articulate a hostility to one issue, say, gun control: she must also oppose government intervention in the economy, education, and residential segregation. Converse then grouped voters according to the level of consistency in their answers. Thus, "ideologues," who comprise about 3.5 percent of voters, are usually the most educated and explicitly cite being liberal or conservative as their guide to voting. At this level, liberals voted only for liberals and knew what liberalism meant. Some 84.5 percent of voters in his sample, however, did not make use of liberal or conservative labels to explain their vote choice, casting serious doubt on the assumptions of spatial theory (1964: 215–18).

Converse's main argument, then, was that "Ideological constraints in belief systems decline with decreasing political information, which is to say that they are present among elites at the 'top' of political systems, or subsystems and disappear rather rapidly as one moves 'downward' into their mass clienteles" (1964: 248). Converse found that "Roughly three-respondents in eight (37%) could supply no meaning for the liberal-conservative distinction, including 8% who attempted to say which party was the more conservative but who gave up on the part of the sequence dealing with meaning" (1964: 220). Between those who could supply no meaning and those who could was a stratum of people who confused liberal and conservative labels with the parties

(1964: 221). Converse also checked to see whether or not voters remained consistent in their positions on the issues over time. In this, he reported, "only about thirteen people out of twenty managed to locate themselves even on the same *side* of the controversy in successive interrogations, when ten out of twenty could have done so by chance alone" (1964: 239; emphasis in original).

If ideology is not a good predictor of vote choice, then what is? When Converse compares the stability of party ID against issue preferences across a four-year time span, he finds on the whole that "The party and affect toward it are more central within the political belief systems of the mass public than are the policy ends that the parties are designed to pursue" (1964: 240–1).

Converse's concept of the "normal vote" is a kind of theoretical vote in which the mass electorate casts their ballots, not based on any rational appraisal of the day's issues or policies, but according to their party ID, that is, as more or less uncritical partisans. The electorate never actually casts a pure "normal vote": Converse intends the concept in the way that Max Weber intended the "ideal type," a baseline reference point against which one might judge successive elections. For example, if there are two major parties in a given country, and 40 percent of voters report over and over again that they are loyalists of Party A, and 60 percent also repeatedly report that they are loyalists of Party B, then that is that country's normal vote, though voters may never cleanly split 40-60 in an actual election. Now if in some future election in year W, the electorate divides 49-51, but then returns to roughly 40-60 in later elections, we might say that W was just a one-off occurrence. According to Converse, this is often what unusual election results mean. If on the other hand, the electorate divides 45-55 in year X, 49-51 in year Y, and 55-45 in year Z, we might say that there is a "realignment" under way, a durable change in the underlying distribution of party loyalties in the electorate.

Here it is important to bear in mind a common caricature of the normal vote and the Michigan model more generally, namely that they expect the distribution of partisan loyalties to be immutable or unchanging. On the contrary, the standard of the normal vote is only a tool to ascertain if realignments in partisan affiliation are in fact afoot (Converse 1966: 28, 30, 33). Converse, in a retrospective piece, in fact writes that he was so excited at the prospect of witnessing an honest-to-goodness realignment in his lifetime that he continually filed away data that seemed to suggest an impending transformation (Converse 2006: 609). Absent any such transformation in the normal distribution of partisan loyalties, however, he was confident enough to assert, "the actual vote in any election, although influenced by short-term forces, is still largely determined by that distribution" (Converse 1966: 18). Thus, in any typical year, the election results are a product of the normal vote primarily (i.e., of uncritical and longstanding partisan loyalties), plus some defection here and there due to short-term forces such as the rise of an issue-du-jour.

Two Contemporary Reassertions

A Straightforward Defense

The disruption of partisan loyalties occasioned by the Civil Rights Movement and the Vietnam War led some analysts to wonder whether voters were as uncritically partisan as the Michigan model had led us to believe. We will review this literature in greater detail alongside spatial theory in the next chapter, but in brief an emerging "revisionist" school of thought argued that a new generation of "issue voters" had started to question their inherited party ID (see pp. 61–4). Accordingly, advocates of the Michigan model rose up in defense. I cover two of the more notable ones here.[1]

In 1989, Eric Smith published *The Unchanging American Voter* in direct response to the issue voter classic, *The Changing American Voter*, by Nie et al. ([1976] 1979). Smith held that the revisionists' findings were based on flawed data and methodology and that, further, there remained significant data to show that voters had not become more sophisticated from 1952 to 1972, not even in what some called the "great leap forward" of 1960 to 1964 (1989: 3).

Revisionists, Smith argued, rely primarily on two indexes.

Borrowed from Converse's essay on the nature of belief systems, these are the index of attitude consistency (attitudes must be consistent with some generally accepted pattern such as all liberal or all conservative) and level of conceptualization (the extent to which one uses abstract terms such as liberalism or conservatism to organize one's beliefs and attitudes). These, however, cannot actually be compared across time for various reasons. In the case of attitude consistency, for example, the question put to respondents in 1960 was different from that asked in 1964 (1989: 3). Voter responses across the two elections therefore cannot be compared. Apart from the problem with the time-series data, the revisionists, Smith adds, attribute trends in the data that don't actually prove political sophistication. For instance, Nie et al. point to an enormous change in the number of "ideologues" in the population between 1960 and 1964, the result apparently of changes in the political environment such as the heated rhetoric over civil rights (1989: 98). Smith cautions, however, that this supposed leap results from the number of ideological statements made about the *candidates*, not the parties. Ideological statements about the parties remained stable from 1960 to 1964 and from 1952 to 1972; it is the voters' ability to correctly connect their ideology (i.e., liberal and conservative) with that of their party, which signals an increase in political sophistication. Ideological statements about candidates are notoriously unreliable and in any case are completely unrelated to political sophistication (1989: 101).

Miller and Shanks' (1996) *The New American Voter* is also a notable reassertion of the Michigan model, in large part because the authors test the relative strength of competing variables taken from all the big debates since Columbia's early voter studies. Miller and Shanks use a "multi-stage" model to identify which variables have the most explanatory power for two outcomes: aggregate election results (i.e., the total vote, who won, who lost) and individual vote choice. The model, which has six stages, is essentially a revised funnel of causality. Stages run from the earliest, long-term, and stable variables like social characteristics and party ID to the most proximate, short-term variables such as impressions of the candidates' personal qualities. Each stage of the analysis tests one or two variables, which correspond to a specific school of thought in the literature. Thus, stage 1 of the analysis tests the Columbia thesis by examining the effects of social characteristics on vote choice and the overall election result. Stage 2 tests party ID (the Michigan thesis) and policy-related predispositions or ideology (the revisionist thesis). Stages 3, 4, and 6 test variables associated with spatial theory, and stage 5 tests the importance of impressions of the candidates' personal qualities (1996: 192).

The authors organize the results by outcome, beginning with aggregate results for the 1992 U.S. presidential election between the Republican incumbent, President George H.W. Bush, and the Democratic challenger, Bill Clinton. The biggest contribution to Clinton's victory, they report, was voter perceptions of current economic conditions, giving a boost to a version of spatial theory ("sociotropic voting"), which holds that voters contemplate not only their own self-interest, but also the good of society as a whole (see p. 67). The second largest effect on the election was party ID, which helped Mr. Clinton since a plurality of voters identified as Democrats. Clinton's advantage in party ID was largely offset, however, by the number of voters who were ideologically predisposed to side with President Bush on policy (1996: 479–80). With respect to individual vote choice, the big story is the persistence of party ID as a critical variable. Indeed, party ID is as powerful a predictor for how an individual will vote as any of the strongest hypotheses since the beginning of the early voter studies. Though generous in giving ample support to other theoretical traditions, Miller and Shanks insist that Michigan has stood the test of time (1996: 483).

The Polarization Debates

The political struggle between U.S. President Bill Clinton and the Republican-controlled Congress in the mid-1990s sparked a second debate, namely, over whether the American electorate was as polarized as their representatives seemed to be. The so-called "polarization debates" are included in this chapter, because their conceptual touchstone is Converse's notion of ideological constraint. That is, to argue that the electorate is polarized pre-supposes that voters who share a conservative position, say, on abortion (i.e., anti-abortion) also share conservative positions on a host of other issues as well like gun control, taxes, affirmative action, immigration, and gay marriage. Likewise, on the other side of the alleged divide, polarization presupposes that voters who are liberal on abortion (i.e., pro-choice) would also be pro-gun control, pro-taxes, pro-affirmative action, pro-immigration, and pro-gay marriage.

An important entrant in the polarization debates was actually a group of sociologists, DiMaggio, Evans, and Bryson (1996). Taking Converse's notion of constraint to mean "the extent to which opinions on any item in an opinion domain . . . are associated with opinions of any other," they find that in fact there is no such "cross-issue contagion" in two sets of survey data, the General Social Survey and the National Election Studies. With the sole exception of social attitudes towards abortion and conservatism, the data suggest convergence – not polarization – on a host of attitudes. Thus, they write, "Americans have become more united in their views on women's role in the public sphere, in their acceptance of racial integration, and in their opinions on matters related to crime and justice" (DiMaggio et al. 1996: 715). These trends suggest a liberal convergence on issues of race and gender and a conservative convergence on crime. To the extent that "Americans have become more divided," it is only, they find, "in their attitudes toward abortion and, less dramatically, in their feelings toward the poor" (DiMaggio et al. 1996: 715).

In contrast, Green et al. (2002) held that American voters are as divided as ever. Looking at the distribution of partisanship in the U.S. population from 1952 to 1998, they find that the balance of partisans to independents in 1996 had returned to levels roughly equivalent to those prior to the Watergate scandal that deposed Richard Nixon in the early 1970s (2002: 14). This number, however, includes those who indicated a party ID (e.g., Strong Republican) but may not have voted. The ratio of partisans to independents increases when they restrict their analysis to those who actually voted: in 1996, 71.4 percent of those voting identified with one of the two parties, and in 1956 it was a comparable 75.9 percent. This general trend is confirmed when they examine who voted for the Democratic presidential candidate by party ID. In the 1952 presidential election, for example, 72.6 percent of Democrats voted for their party's candidate compared to 33.5 percent of independents, and just 3.8 percent of Republicans; forty years later Bill Clinton carried an even higher proportion of Democrats. Thus, 82.4 percent of Democrats voted for Mr. Clinton in 1992, compared to 42.3 percent of independents, and 8.9 percent of Republicans (2002: 15). All of this is to suggest that if we take the Michigan model's concept of party ID as an index of polarization, then we can say without much hesitation that the American electorate is polarized.

Note, however, that for Green et al. voters are polarized so long as they identify with different parties: whether voters actually disagree on the issues is of little moment. In fact, it is theoretically possible for two voters who agree on every issue to be counted as polarized in Green et al.'s model, so long as they have different party IDs and vote accordingly. This assumption is at variance with that of DiMaggio et al., who claim exactly the opposite: that public opinion can only be said to be polarized if there is divergence on a broad set of issues.

Baldassarri and Gelman's 2008 article (also from sociology) split the difference between these two poles. Again returning to Converse's concept of ideological constraint, they find that contemporary American voters are much better than they used to be at "matching their issue preferences with their party ideology." For example, they know "pro-choice" on the issue of abortion goes with the Democratic Party. However, they also find that "their level of issue constraint has remained essentially stable – and low," meaning that the average American voter tends to be liberal on some things and conservative on others. They take this to mean that "issue partisanship is not due to higher ideological coherence." American voters have not developed more sophisticated or internally consistent belief systems (2008: 411).

Schema Theory

"Schema" is a term borrowed from psychology to denote the strategies that voters use to simplify political information, which can be complex and massive in amount, especially during elections. Schema theory emerged in political science to unlock the "black box" (Lodge and Stroh 1993) of party ID – that is, to identify and explain the psychological processes that make party ID such a critical determinant of vote choice. Over time, however, schema theory has turned increasingly to the ways in which voters use symbolic or simplified information to evaluate candidates and parties; how this information is used in individual vote choice has become less important. There are various streams of research in this general area, and I review them here under two subcategories: "symbolic politics" and "information processing" (sometimes called "political psychology").

Symbolic Politics

A foundational piece in the symbolic politics literature is Sears et al.'s (1979) study of white opposition to busing in the 1970s United States. Busing was an attempt to institutionalize the gains of the Civil Rights Movement, which toppled the doctrine that the U.S. Constitution permitted separate facilities for blacks and whites, so long as they were equal. To counteract racial segregation in American schools, the courts ordered segregated white communities, typically in the suburbs, to "bus" their children to schools in segregated communities of color, typically in inner cities, and vice versa. Court-ordered busing met with stiff resistance from whites in both the North and South and became a central issue in the 1972 presidential election between the Republican incumbent Richard Nixon, who opposed busing, and Democratic Senator George McGovern, who favored it. Sears et al. set out to determine the degree to which spatial theory and other rational actor theories explained this resistance.

The authors identify three problems with existing studies, whose core assumption is that voters form attitudes and opinions

47

by calculating the cost and benefit of certain policies or events to their livelihood. First, studies based on aggregate-level (e.g., state-wide or national) data on public opinion cannot tell us whether the *individuals* who are actually hurt or harmed by, say, an economic downturn are in fact the ones whose votes are swayed in the appropriate direction (e.g., from the governing party during the downturn to the opposition). Next, and in a related vein, studies that make claims about the divergent interests and attitudes of "competing" groups are problematic, because interests vary widely within large groups (e.g., women), and often those who feel strongly about a certain issue are not necessarily those who are most affected by it. For instance, they suggest that the staunchest advocates of gender equality tend not to be poor, uneducated housewives in abusive marriages, but more affluent, college-educated single women. Studies that examine the effect of policy issues on personal life are problematic for similar reasons. Thus, the authors point out that personal experiences with crime tend not to have an impact on voters' attitudes towards law enforcement (1979: 370).

As an alternative to rational actor theories, Sears et al. propose the "symbolic politics" model. In order to demonstrate the authors' shared lineage with the Michigan tradition, I quote their definition of this model at length:

> According to this theory, people acquire in early life standing predispositions which influence their adult perceptions and attitudes. In adulthood, then, they respond in a highly affective way to symbols which resemble the attitude objects to which similar emotional responses were conditioned or associated in earlier life . . . One's relevant personal "stake" in the issue is an emotional, symbolic one; it triggers long-held, habitual responses. So, for example, the importance of political symbols such as "integration," "blacks," or "Harlem" is that they evoke underlying predispositions, such as the person's racial intolerance or prejudice. (1979: 371)

As with party ID, then, symbolic politics are said to tap into the emotional or affective predispositions that are formed early in life. To the degree that voters perceive a "personal stake" in an issue, that stake has less to do with the actual cost or benefit to their personal livelihood (e.g., being ordered to bus their child), and more to do with longstanding habits of the heart such as racial prejudice. Thus, the party–society linkage occurs when parties send out symbolic cues that bind, as an enzyme does to a substrate, to longstanding emotional associations in the electorate.

In order to test the symbolic politics model against rational actor theories, Sears et al. use individual-level survey data from the 1972 presidential election. If rational actor theories are correct, then whites whose communities have been ordered to bus should cast a busing-based vote, whereas those who are not personally affected by busing should cast a vote based on other issues. Sears et al. find that having a "personal stake" in busing was not a significant predictor of whites' voting behavior in the 1972 election. That is, whites who lived in school districts that were *not* ordered to bus, were just as likely as those who did live in such districts to vote against busing. Far more predictive were "symbolic attitudes (racial intolerance and political conservatism) on opposition to busing." They add, "'Busing' has become a highly charged symbol of race mixing and of change in the status quo, and so it seems to trigger most opposition from the usual opponents of such social changes, rather than any unique reaction from people who might be personally affected" (1979: 369, 381–2). For Sears et al., then, it is the deeply entrenched affective predispositions of the people that explain voting behavior, not voters' rational adjudication of cost and benefit.

A direct descendant of Sears' research is Rabinowitz and Macdonald's (1989) "directional theory" of issue voting. Like many of the preceding works, directional theory is a response to rational actor theories, and above all Anthony Downs' spatial theory (see pp. 58–61). Rabinowitz and Macdonald assume that voters operate on very low levels of information. Therefore the Downsian claim that a voter might know exactly where s/he and the parties stand on a given issue is in essence a fiction. Instead, an individual's preferences are said to be "diffuse" or imprecise. Voters are reliably aware of only two things. First, they know the general "direction" of their preferences: whether they are for or against something. Second, they have some sense of the "intensity" of their support or opposition. To return to a previous example, voters know whether or not they are pro- or anti-war, and they are aware of how strongly they feel that way (1989: 94).

Directional theory's assumptions for voting behavior run counter to the second major implication of spatial theory, namely, that in a society where voter preferences cluster around the ideological center, the centrist party or candidate holds the dominant position and is therefore likely to win the most votes. In contrast, Rabinowitz and Macdonald propose two alternative theorems about the dynamics of electoral competition. The first theorem is that in a "normal" or centrist distribution of voters, any position is equally competitive provided that the parties stay within a "region of acceptability," where a party's views are not dismissed as "crazy" or beyond the pale. A neo-Nazi or communist party would probably fall outside the region of acceptability for most American voters, for example. The second theorem is that when the electorate has a clear directional preference (i.e., is not clustered in the center), the candidate with the most extreme position within the region of acceptability is the most highly rewarded. The reason is that while a voter may not feel as intensely as extremist Candidate A does on an issue, provided that she shares the same general direction or point of view (e.g., pro-war), she will vote for Candidate A, because she has a clearer idea about where A stands than she does about centrist Candidate B. In other words, A gets her vote, because A deploys the political symbol for that issue better than B (1989: 109).

Their analysis of U.S. presidential elections from 1972 to 1984 suggests that with the possible exception of votes for President Carter in 1980, directional theory explains more of the variation in individual voting behavior than the spatial model. Previous studies of elections to the U.S. House of Representatives corroborate these results. One study found that "the losing candidate was closer on the average to the mean voter than was the winning candidate." Another analysis found that "representatives tended to be significantly more extreme than the mean voter" (1989: 102–7, 111).

If Rabinowitz and Macdonald are correct, then the goals and challenges of parties are different from those implied by Downs. Whereas a party's goal according to spatial theory should be to tack to the center or wherever voters cluster, in directional theory "the goal is to be the candidate who makes the most effective use of the symbol." And whereas for Downs a party's key challenge is to detect and then pitch to the median voter, for Rabinowitz and Macdonald the challenge is to stay within the region of acceptability (1989: 109).

Information Processing

Scholars of "information processing" are different from their counterparts in the wider partisan voter approach, because they assume that voters use information, but they are similar to their colleagues in insisting that voters do not process such information in a strictly "rational" way. Rahn's work on the appraisal of candidates is a case in point. Rahn et al. (1990) describe schema as organized structures of knowledge (I have described them above as knowledge "strategies") that one uses to make assessments not only of candidates, but also of people in general. These structures are generic and stable symbolic terms such as "integrity" or "reliability," which help voters simplify the information environment as they form "images" of the competing candidates. In contrast to some who suggest that only sophisticated voters use schema, they argue that people use schema everyday. Thus, they write, "we will argue that individual differences in political expertise or interest ... should not result in different candidate appraisal processes because all citizens have sufficient practice in evaluating others in the course of their daily lives" (Rahn et al. 1990: 138–40).

Their model therefore has four assumptions. First, although voters are capable of forming impressions based on party ID, Rahn et al. assume that voters can also form images of candidates in much the same that they "form impressions of people encountered in everyday life." Secondly, and as a result, "most voters are capable of distinguishing between the political characteristics of candidates and the candidates' personal qualities." Next, voters develop "feelings" about candidates as part of this process. For example, they can be proud of the candidate because of her or his supposed strength in world affairs, though it might stem primarily from the fact that s/he is a war veteran. Finally, and as a result of the foregoing, they assume "voting is a relatively uncomplicated decision for most people" and thus does not require a high level of sophistication (1990: 141–2).

Lodge and Stroh (1993) contend that the Columbia (see pp. 19–22) and Michigan models are both "black box" models of candidate evaluation: they assume that voters use their memories to form evaluations (albeit in different ways) but do not explain the actual process by which memories go in and evaluations come out. The problem with black box models goes even further than that, because memory-based evaluations, even if we assume that they occur, have very little credibility. Memories, they point out, are often obscured by stereotyping and "posthoc" justifications (i.e., people alter their memories *after the fact* to justify why they like and dislike others). As in Rahn et al., then, their emphasis is on mental processes, not the prediction of vote choice.

To avoid the pitfalls of black box models, Lodge and Stroh abandon "the strong memory-based assumptions characteristic of political science models of evaluation." Their alternative model assumes that the voter stores an impression of a candidate as it is forming and forgets the rest. The voter does not *recall* the information after the fact. On election day, the voter takes a tally of all her impressions and proceeds accordingly. This is why, for example, people can often tell you that they really liked a book or a movie, but cannot recount the specific reasons for their appraisal (1993: 227–8). Note that what is stored is the "affective" or emotional "value" of the encounter, "not the bits and pieces of information originally contributed to the evaluation" (1993: 229).

The work of Lodge, Stroh, and Rahn dovetails with Popkin's concept of "low-information rationality." Popularly known as "gut reasoning," the concept denotes "a method of combining, in an economical way, learning and information from past experiences, daily life, the media, and political campaigns" (1991: 7). Like the two preceding works, then, Popkin's assumes that people are "reasoning voters" to the degree that they make use of information in rendering political evaluations, but that they do not reason in the way that rational actors would. Instead, voters mix selective bits of information or "cues" with their own life experience and values to complete an impression about a candidate. Popkin writes,

> To study the cues, or information shortcuts, that people use in voting is to study how people supply themselves with information that fills in their pictures of candidates and governments. Cues enable voters to call on beliefs about people and government from which they can generate or recall scenarios, or "scripts," as they are called in psychology. A little information can go a long way . . . They can absorb a few cues and then complete their picture with the help of their "default values." (1991: 16)

What do cues look like and how might they elicit gut reactions from voters? On a campaign tour of New York City, for instance, Senator George McGovern, the 1972 Democratic nominee for president, ordered a kosher hot dog at a Jewish deli, only to ask for milk to go with it (a non-kosher mix) (1991: 2). Though not a substantive policy position, Jewish voters, Popkin speculates, likely took this moment as a cue that Mr. McGovern did not know the culture of the people whose votes he sought. Similarly, in 1982 when the unemployment rate in the United States was at its highest in 50 years, First Lady Nancy Reagan served dinner at the White House on a $250,000 set of china (1991: 103). If McGovern's tour of the Big Apple signaled that the candidate was a touch waspy, the later episode served as a cue to the voting public that the Reagan administration was out of touch with regular people (1991: 103).

Popkin is careful to point out, however, that campaign events at delis and dinner parties should not be divorced from *rhetorical* symbols. That is, candidate statements are not just "issue positions" (1991: 6). To tell a joint session of Congress that "either you are with us, or you are with the terrorists," as President George W. Bush did in 2001, is not a policy briefing. It is a symbolic act meant to tie putative character flaws such as "weakness" and "lack of resolve" to the opposition.

As research on information processing has evolved, some scholars have sought to uncover how party politics manifests itself chemically in the brain. A well-known example is a neuropsychological study called *The Political Brain* by Drew Westen (2007). The main target of the book is once again the concept of the "dispassionate mind," which undergirds so much of the scholarship in psychology and political science. The viewpoint that "we are largely rational actors, who make important decisions by weighing the evidence and calculating the costs and benefits," Westen argues, "bears no relation to how the mind and brain actually work." The political brain is instead an "emotional brain" (Westen 2007: ix–x, xv).

The evidence for this alternative viewpoint was an experiment on the psychological dynamics of the 2004 U.S. presidential election between the Republican incumbent George W. Bush and the Democratic challenger, U.S. Senator John Kerry. Westen and his collaborators asked 15 Democrats and 15 Republicans to rate the level of inconsistency in six sets of paired contradictory statements from Kerry, Bush, and politically neutral male figures (e.g., Tom Hanks), where 1 (one) signified that the respondent strongly disagreed that the two statements were contradictory and 4 (four) signified that the respondent strongly agreed (Westen 2007: xi–xii). Simply put, Westen's team wanted to see if people could be objectively critical when the leader of their own party contradicted himself.

It turns out they can't. The respondents had no problem identifying the contradiction in the opposition candidate's statements, but they insisted that their own candidate had *not* contradicted himself. The early voting studies observed a similar dynamic, so that much is not exactly groundbreaking, but what is fascinating about Westen's account are his insights into the neurological circuitry involved in this process. The brain appears to register the conflict between the statements of their favored candidate and shows signs of emotional distress. When that happens, the brain does two things in quick succession. First, it begins to shut down distress by turning off "the spigot of unpleasant emotion." Second, it then quickly turns on the circuits of positive emotion, giving partisans "a jolt of positive reinforcement for their biased reasoning" (Westen 2007: xiii–xiv).

But if people develop emotional attachments to parties, then how exactly do such attachments get triggered? Westen's answer echoes that of the rest of the partisan voter approach. Crucial to playing to the political brain are "primes." In a discussion of playing the so-called "race card," Westen contends that the response of whites to race in the polling booth depends on which primes political parties send. When southern whites in particular hear that they are backwater bigots, they bristle and tend to oppose racially progressive candidates. On the other hand, when they are primed by a discourse of injustice, poverty, and the concrete realities of racial discrimination, Westen argues, whites in the North and South respond with sympathy and solidarity (Westen 2007: 227–30). The party–society linkage therefore takes hold when the party sends the "correct" prime to the voter; if the party sends the wrong prime, then the linkage fails.

*

By way of conclusion, we return, as we did in the previous chapter, to the main arguments of the book. First, to understand the field, one must recognize that the wide-ranging interdisciplinary debate over the texture and determinants of democratic party politics includes sociology. With respect to this chapter, the partisan voter approach very clearly emerged in direct response to the Columbia sociological model (see pp. 19–22). It was only later, as the theoretical framework matured, that Michigan social scientists turned to another nemesis: the issue voter (see pp. 57–8). Second, I have argued that there is no one approach to this subject in sociology. The sociologists embroiled in the polarization debates provide strong evidence on this point. Significantly, we also find in this chapter the first caricature of sociology as being socially deterministic. That is, if sociologists are pigeon-holed even today as having one, instead of several, perspectives on democratic party politics, then it is partially due to the early advocates of the partisan voter.

The caricature underscores my third argument, which is that jurisdictional squabbles between political scientists and sociologists obscure more than they illuminate. Indeed, the partisan and social voter approaches share at least two things in common: the analytical emphasis on individual vote choice and the methodological commitment to survey data, which takes the individual as the primary unit of analysis. Further, DiMaggio et al. and Baldassarri and Gelman, sociologists all, use Converse's concept of ideological constraint to stake their claims in the polarization debates. My fourth argument is that party-centered approaches are not in conversation with voter-centered approaches. Michigan's interlocutors were not the advocates of party-centered approaches, but those of other voter-centered approaches, initially the social voter, and later, the issue voter. Lastly, the intersection among party, state, and society is under-theorized as it is in the wider field, partly because of the presumed separation of parties from everything else. The partisan voter approach, like the social voter, is silent on the state, and has little to say about parties as organizations. The key Michigan variable, party ID, has to do with an individual's upbringing as a child in a partisan household. Party, on this account, is a remote organization, whose name has emotional and symbolic significance, not primarily because of what parties do (though schema theory is occasionally an exception here), but because of what families do.

3

The Issue Voter

As I have hinted in the preceding chapter, the concept of "the issue voter" represented a challenge to the partisan voter approach (see pp. 32–3). Its proponents might meaningfully be divided into two broad camps: those who were associated with the Michigan tradition (see pp. 35–42), and those who were not. The former camp consists of two groups. One, called the "revisionists," held that while uncritical adherence to inherited party ID may have accurately described the behavior of American voters during the New Deal, it did not hold true for new voters who came of age during the 1960s. This new cohort of voters, whose parents were the children of Depression era voters, were not only removed from the economic traumas of the past, but also more educated than the previous two cohorts of voters. They were, in other words, more open to political persuasion in the context of new events and issues such as the Vietnam War and civil rights (Key 1966; Pomper 1972; Nie et al. [1976] 1979). A closely related group consists of the "socialization" school of realignment theory, a research tradition dedicated to explaining sharp and durable shifts in partisan allegiances (see especially Beck 1974; Carmines and Stimson 1989; Carmines et al. 1987).

Spatial theory, by contrast, originated with the work of Hotelling (1929), Smithies (1941), Downs (1957), and Black ([1958] 1963), and thus had its own theoretical lineage, distinct from the Michigan model. A key assumption of this tradition is that voters are always rational actors; they are not blind partisans for a generation and

57

rational in the next as the revisionists imply. Voters have issue preferences and choose candidates whose preferences are closest to their own. Within this broad framework, there are at least five streams of research. Downs, in the classic programmatic statement of spatial theory, assumed that voters pick the candidate closest to them on a "liberal to conservative" scale based on how *they expect* the candidate will serve their own *self*-interest. This is called "prospective" (future-oriented) and "egotropic" (self-interested) voting in "one-dimensional space" (single issue voting). Additionally, to the degree that political candidates had any autonomy at all, classical spatial theory assumed that they simply positioned themselves where voters clustered. In contrast, Fiorina (1981) held that voting is fundamentally a retrospective act, in which voters appraise an incumbent's past performance in government. Kinder and Kiewiet (1981), pioneers of the "sociotropic" school, assume that voters evaluate candidates based on issues pertaining to the well-being of society as a whole (e.g., economic prosperity). Melvin Hinich and his associates explained how voters confront multi-issue campaigns and broadened the scope of candidate behavior (for overviews, see Enelow and Hinich 1984 and Merrill and Grofman 1999). Finally, a few scholars have worked to meet the challenge of Rabinowitz and Macdonald's directional theory by synthesizing it with spatial theory (see, for example, Iversen 1994 and Merrill and Grofman 1999). Both the spatial and revisionist traditions are elaborated below.

Classical Spatial Theory

Spatial theory has several applications, but like the Columbia and Michigan models (see pp. 19–22, 35–42), it is also a preeminent theory of individual vote choice. Its central claim, and a key point of contention as we saw in the previous chapter, is that voters choose parties and candidates, whose policy or issue preferences are *closest* to their own. There are four assumptions. The first is the variable distribution of the population, meaning that voters' policy preferences are not identical to one another but are rather spread across an ideological continuum from left to right or liberal to conservative. The second assumption is that parties are similarly ordered from left to right. The third is relative ideological immobility, meaning that voters' preferences are assumed not to change. The fourth and related assumption is "peaked political preferences" for all voters: each voter has an ideal point on the left-to-right continuum at which their policy preference is best satisfied. This also suggests that the voter will choose the candidate or party who comes closest to this ideal point.

For example, let us assume that in the wake of a natural disaster, there are five positions on funding disaster relief: socialists in the legislature prefer to increase funding by $300 billion; liberals prefer an increase of $150 billion; moderate conservatives from areas hardest hit by the disaster want to keep funding at existing levels; moderate conservatives outside the disaster zone prefer to decrease funding by $150 billion; and far right conservatives prefer a cut in funding of $300 billion. Let us assume further that you are a voter from the disaster zone who prefers an increase in funding of $100 billion, and that the two candidates in your district are a liberal and a moderate conservative, who support their respective factions' positions in the debate over disaster relief funding. According to spatial theory, you would vote for the liberal, because the difference between your preference and hers is $50 billion, whereas the difference between your preference and that of the moderate conservative is $100 billion.

Unlike the social and partisan voter approaches, spatial theory's assumptions about individual vote choice inform a related theory of party behavior. If voters are attracted to parties that are least distant from them, then parties will rationally try to discern where most voters are located on a given issue, and, provided that voters cluster around one position, parties will pitch their message as close to that position as possible. Anthony Downs' (1957) foundational synthesis of spatial theory is anchored in early studies of firm and consumer behavior. The latter predicted that two competing firms in a given town will make their products as similar, and relocate their storefronts geographically as close, to each other as possible to maximize market share (Hotelling 1929), while not diluting the distinctiveness of their product or moving so far in the opposite direction as to alienate their die-hard clientele (Smithies 1941). Thus, McDonald's and Burger King typically sell comparable lines of fast food (e.g., Big Mac versus Whopper) and are often found on opposite sides of the same highway to capture the largest number of customers. However, the two competitors' products are not identical (e.g., Burger King insists that its burgers are "flame broiled"), and neither relocates to the other's side of the street for fear that crossing the highway might make transportation costs too high for their old customers. Similarly, if polling data reveal that a plurality of voters favors military intervention in Iran, then a party whose constituents include those who oppose war under any circumstances will not rule out military invention so as to attract the plurality of voters, but neither will it commit to a unilateral invasion so as to retain the loyalty of the pacifists in their ranks (Downs 1957: 114–17).

The distribution of voters' policy preferences along the political spectrum, like the distribution of consumers in a local market, therefore shapes how parties will behave. Parties are not exactly passive, but neither are they the decisive actors in democratic politics. Three distributions are possible, each of which influences (a) the number of parties that are able to effectively compete in a given representative democracy, and (b) the political culture of that democracy. In a democracy where there is a "normal" distribution of voters – that is, where most of the voters tend to cluster around the middle – there are typically two major parties that vie for power in a political culture that is "moderate" or "centrist" in nature. Under these conditions, Downs predicts the McDonald's/ Burger King outcome described above: the two parties will rationally seek to resemble one another in order to capture the "median voter," but remain somewhat distinct in order to retain the loyalty of their "base."[1] Under these conditions, the median voter is the issue position on the left-to-right spectrum that cannot be beaten in a majority vote. In a democracy where there is a "bimodal" distribution of voters – that is, where half the electorate is clustered at one extreme and the remainder is gathered at the other – there are once again two major parties, but they operate in an environment of intense polarization, sometimes teetering on the brink of civil war. In such cases, there is no rational incentive for the parties to resemble one another, because there are few if any voters in the middle. A "win" under these circumstances is not truly a national victory, but a question of who can best preach to their own choir. Each party will therefore seek to differentiate itself as much as possible from the other. Finally, a democracy whose voters are distributed equally across three or more political camps encourages multiparty systems to take hold. The political culture of such a community, while tending less toward civil war, may be described as factious and unstable, because political parties have little rational incentive to reach out beyond their respective constituencies. In order to govern, political adversaries must enter into parliamentary coalitions that are often brought down in short order by internal strife (Downs 1957: 118–22).

The Revisionists

Unlike the early spatial theorists, who shared a model of vote choice and party behavior, the revisionists were more theoretically eclectic and, furthermore, were tied in one way or another to the Michigan model. For example, V.O. Key, once a champion of the early Michigan voter studies, became uncomfortable with the image, propounded by his erstwhile protégés, of the voter as a fool. In the hands of Michigan social scientists, voting became "an almost purely deterministic act" that could be predicted on the basis of the voter's occupation, residence, religion, national origins, and political attitudes (Key 1966: 4–5). In contrast to this image, Key famously insisted that "The voice of the people is but an echo" (1966: 3), for the choices they make at the ballot box are "a selective reflection from among the alternatives and outlooks presented to them . . . If the people can choose only from among rascals, they are certain to choose a rascal" (1966: 2–3). Given the poverty of choices, information, and clarity in front of him, then, the voter behaves just "about as rationally and responsibly as we should expect" (1966: 7).

Drawing on data from U.S. presidential campaigns between 1936 and 1960, Key examined the behavior of three types of voters: the standpatters who stay with the same party through two successive elections, the switchers who defect from the party they voted for in the previous election, and new voters, who include those who come of voting age and "in-and-out" voters (those who were non-voters in the previous election) (1966: 8, 16). Key finds some support for Campbell et al.'s concept of party ID, as the "Standpatters stay by the party even though they agree with the opposition party." However, he also finds that issue preferences can either reinforce or undermine party loyalty. "Those who agree with their party are most inclined to stay with it," he writes, whereas "Those whose policy preference conflicts with their party voting record are most likely to defect." These findings, he says, are "consistent with the supposition that voters, or at least a large number of them, are moved by perceptions and appraisals of policy and performance" (1966: 150).

Similarly, Gerald Pomper (1972), in a classic essay titled, "From Confusion to Clarity," analyzed the relationship between voter preferences on six policy issues on the one hand and partisan variables on the other (party ID, awareness of the difference between parties on the six issues, and consensus in the electorate about the position of the two parties). The six issues were federal aid to education, government provision of medical care, government guarantee of full employment, federal enforcement of fair employment and fair housing, federal enforcement of school integration, and foreign aid (1972: 416–17). In contrast to Converse's claims about the intellectual disorganization of the mass electorate, Pomper finds that from 1956 to 1968, "all segments of the population displayed considerable political learning" in three areas. First, voters' issue preferences matched their party ID. Second, more people were aware of the differences between the parties on these issues. And third, there was greater consensus on where each party stood. Further, Pomper found that political learning in the 1960s occurred on these issues across age groups, race, region, and educational attainment (1972: 420–1).

More important to the revisionist challenge than the work of

Pomper and Key, however, was Nie et al.'s ([1976] 1979) book, *The Changing American Voter*. The tone of the book is notably conciliatory toward the Michigan model, suggesting that Campbell et al. (1960) captured accurately the stable, unquestioned, partisan loyalties of the 1950s (see pp. 36–8). Beginning in the 1960s, however, the American electorate changed: it became "more politically aroused, more detached from political parties than at any time in the past forty years, and deeply dissatisfied with the political process" ([1976] 1979: 1–2). Nie et al. trace this overall change to two factors. The first factor is the emergence of new issues such as civil rights, the Vietnam War, the urban riots, the Watergate scandal, and the economic recession of the 1970s. The second is the emergence of a new cohort of voters with only second-hand attachment to the partisan allegiances of the New Deal era.

The early voter studies, the authors concede, were right to argue that political attitudes originated with early socialization in the family; where they erred was in taking the added step of suggesting that these attitudes were more or less permanent. Such a claim is indefensible from a methodological standpoint, because the survey of the electorate in Campbell et al.'s *The American Voter*, like all such samples, was only a snapshot of political attitudes in the 1950s. Political attitudes might very well change from year to year ([1976] 1979: 7). Thus, *TAV* found that the average American citizen was only marginally involved in politics, ideologically unsophisticated and confused, essentially satisfied with the political system, and uncritically loyal to one of the major parties. In contrast, Nie et al. found, especially among new voters, an educated and politically exercised average citizen, who is more attuned to the issues and less beholden to their inherited party ID ([1976] 1979: 15, 18, 23, 28, 35, 46).

Their theoretical framework is essentially that of the socialization theory of realignment, inaugurated by Beck (1974) and later elaborated in the punctuated equilibrium models of Carmines et al. (1987) and Carmines and Stimson (1989). Party ID, Nie et al. argue, forms in response to the issues of the day, but once partisan loyalties take hold, they become more or less fixed. This is the stage at which Campbell et al. took their sample. However, these loyalties eventually fade or at least become second-hand, as those who inherit their party ID from their parents and their parents' parents become removed from the short-term events and issues that defined the realigning generation. Still, old party identifications are not likely to change unless "potent new issues, and a new generation of voters" emerge, in which case, "the stability of party commitments is shattered" ([1976] 1979: 46).

Similarly, Beck (1974) argued that the process of party-voter realignment was an affair of three related groups of voters. The first group is the cohort who came of age in "a realigning phase" (e.g., a civil war, a severe economic downturn). The partisanship of this "realignment generation" is likely to have stronger intellectual underpinnings and loyalties than any other age group. The second group consists of those who inherited their party ID from the realignment generation: these are the "children of realignment," who, while not having been born during the realigning phase, nevertheless were exposed to intense political conflict through their parents across the proverbial dinner table. The third group consists of the "children of normal politics," that is, the group who inherit their party ID second-hand through their parents, who themselves did not live through the trauma of realignment (1974: 206–7). It is this third group that is most vulnerable to the influences of short-term events and issues of the day, and thus, "provide the dynamic element to American electoral politics" (1974: 205). Accordingly, we might say that Nie et al.'s snapshot sample consists in the generation coming of age in the 1960s and 1970s, the "children of normal politics."

Spatial Theory Revisited

Though some scholarly observers agreed broadly with the revisionist claim that voters were not as irrational as the partisan voter approach insisted, they remained unsatisfied with a disorganization of another kind, namely, the absence of an alternative revisionist theory that could stand up to the Michigan model. This problem, along with various methodological gaps, was put on display in a scathing essay by Michael Margolis (1977), titled, "From Confusion to Confusion," which was a reply on behalf of the Michigan model to Gerald Pomper. Accordingly, the emerging voices in the field turned to spatial theory, not just to re-apply it, but also to revise several of its underlying assumptions. First, as Stokes (1963) famously pointed out, spatial theory assumes that voters' issue preferences are ordered on a one-dimensional continuum from left to right. Second, the scope of candidate behavior was limited to merely following voters to where they clustered in great numbers. The next assumption is that people vote based on how well they expect a candidate or party will serve their interests. Voting is, in other words, assumed to be a future-oriented or "prospective" practice. The last assumption is that people vote according to their own self-interest. This is called "egotropic" voting.

Melvin Hinich and his associates revised the first two assumptions. Multidimensional issue modeling originates with the work of Davis and Hinich (1966) and is expanded in Enelow and Hinich (1984). Without going into great mathematical detail, their aim in each case is to locate a dominant median point in two-dimensional space (i.e., a space with x and y axes) that cannot be beaten in a majority vote. This is an advance on classical spatial theory, which seeks to locate the median voter on a single axis of preferences ordered from left to right and is therefore only able to predict voting behavior provided that the voters dispose of one issue at a time. With respect to candidate autonomy, the Hinich team also employs spatial theory to explain why some candidates frame their opponents as "out of touch with the mainstream," whereas others downplay their differences with their opponents. The former case, they argue, is typically the stance of the incumbent. In that case, the latter is trying to increase the "perceived policy distance" between the candidates, so as to render her or him unacceptable to the median voter. To counter the incumbent play, the challenger seeks correspondingly to shrink the perceived policy distance between him and the incumbent (Enelow and Hinich 1984: 51–2; see also Enelow and Hinich 1982). The 2012 U.S. presidential election between Democratic incumbent Barack Obama and Republican challenger Mitt Romney is a case in point. For most of the campaign Mr. Obama painted his opponent as an extreme right-wing ideologue, whose only goal was to enrich the top 1 percent of American wage earners. In contrast, from the first presidential debate onward, Mr. Romney insisted that he agreed with the president to some degree on taxes, health care, and women's reproductive health, thus re-positioning himself in the mainstream.

Morris Fiorina's 1981 book is the foundational work in "retrospective" (as opposed to "prospective") voting. Fiorina is careful to point out that he is not the first to suggest that people look backward when casting their ballots. Another is V.O. Key's (1966) "reward-punishment" thesis. Fiorina calls this the "traditional" variant of retrospective voting, because the voter does not care about the different means of achieving an ultimate end as long as it is achieved. For example, the parents of a soldier may want the government to end a war, so their son can return home. How the government achieves this end is less important than whether or not the incumbent has brought the war to a close. If s/he hasn't, then the voter's impulse will be to "throw the rascal out." Fiorina's variant, which is based on spatial theory, suggests that the voter uses a candidate's or party's previous policies as an indication or clue of future policy direction. The voter pays attention to the party's track record, because the means matter as much to her or him as the end pursued. To draw on the previous example, another parent may care how the government winds down the war, in which case the voter's choice is based on her agreement or disagreement with the candidates on policy. Fiorina's posture here is synthetic. Key's traditional framework, he says, applies in elections or on issues in which voters make no distinction between policy means and ends; the vote is based entirely on whether the end has been achieved and one's life thereby improved or worsened. Spatial theory is right when there is a distinction between policy means and ends. This is a different rational decision-making process. The voter discerns which policy s/he agrees with more (a classic assumption of spatial theory), not just the incumbent's past performance writ large (1981: 12–13). Accordingly, Fiorina's model of retrospective voting is one in which individual vote choice "depends on the notion that citizens monitor party promises and performances over time . . . and rely on this core of previous experience when they assign responsibility for current societal conditions and evaluate ambiguous platforms designed to deal with uncertain futures" (1981: 83).

If the revisionists' problem is the absence of a coherent theoretical framework, then for Kinder and Kiewiet (1981), the answer to that gap is not a theory based on "pocketbook politics." The latter suggests that people vote purely according to economic self-interest. In their alternative, "sociotropic prediction," Kinder and Kiewiet assume instead that the voter "in reaching political preferences . . . is influenced most of all by the nation's economic condition. Purely sociotropic citizens vote according to the country's pocketbook, not their own." This is why the majority party is typically punished at the polls during economic downturns, whereas the party that presides over flush economic times is typically returned to office. This is not to say, however, that theirs is an altruistic model of voting behavior. Indeed, Kinder and Kiewiet caution that "sociotropic voting may be totally self-interested." For example, a small business owner may view the government's superior handling of the economy as beneficial to his own well-being, since general economic prosperity means that consumers will be able to buy his goods or services (1981: 132).

The internal arguments over prospective, egotropic, and multidimensional issue voting were not the only objects on spatial theory's radar, however. After the initial challenge posed by Stokes and the Michigan model, perhaps the most important attack on spatial theory came from Rabinowitz and Macdonald's directional theory of issue voting, which, as we have seen, was published in 1989. The 1990s therefore witnessed various attempts at synthesizing the major findings of spatial and directional theory. Iversen (1994), for example, held that such a synthesis is required to account for voting behavior in *multiparty* systems. Recall that when the electorate has a clear directional preference (e.g., a majority opposes "austerity" cuts to government programs), then directional theory predicts that the more strident candidates who share the same preference are the most highly rewarded, whereas centrist candidates who pander to spatial theory's mythical median voter typically lose. Iversen argues that neither theory is fully right or wrong. The key (as I read him) is to bracket spatial theory's emphasis on the median voter and foreground its attention to the policy distance between voter and party. In this way, he finds that in multiparty systems "voters prefer parties that offer clear and intense political alternatives," as Rabinowitz and Macdonald predict, but also "turn away from parties that deviate too radically from voters' own stated policy positions" very much as spatial theorists have long argued (1994: 45). Similarly, Merrill and Grofman (1999) find that in both two-party and multiparty systems, parties are neither identical nor extremely divergent from one another. They call this empirical consistency across their three cases, the United States, France, and Norway, "moderate extremism," and hold that a unified model incorporating direction, spatial proximity, as well as party ID is necessary to understand the mixture of factors that give rise to it (1999: 4, 40–7).

Realignment Theory: A Brief Word

In 2000, the Yale political scientist David Mayhew published an annual review article that is widely viewed as having sounded the death knell of realignment theory, the research tradition devoted to examining what V.O. Key once called "sharp and durable" shifts in partisan loyalties among the electorate (1955: 11). The classic example of a realignment is the New Deal, in which a large swath of the American public switched their political allegiance from the Republican to the Democratic party during the Great Depression. To the degree that realignments occur, Mayhew claimed, one need only pay attention to unforeseen events and valence issues (which, to repeat, hinge on government stewardship of economic prosperity, etc.) to understand why voters sometimes abandon their political parties for good. No theory, least of all the elaborate infrastructure supporting realignment theory, is necessary to explain why people defect from a party that presided over a cataclysm of Depression-like proportions (Mayhew 2000: 462, 471).

As Abramson et al. (2010) point out, however, Mayhew's

claims are based on a caricature that reduces realignment theory to just one perspective in what is actually a large and diverse body of work. I would add that Mayhew's critique is even more problematic, because short-term events and issues – factors that Mayhew suggests realignment scholars have difficulty digesting – are part of nearly *all* theories of realignment. Indeed, I will argue here that the competing schools of thought on realignment attempt to explain, albeit in different ways, the shift from stable partisan voting patterns (one might call this party ID) to issue voting in the midst of transformative events. It is for this reason that I include the realignment tradition in this chapter.

What Mayhew finds most objectionable is the "critical realignment" perspective of Burnham (1970), Sundquist (1983), Brady (1988), and others. These scholars contend that some form of strain or tension gradually increases in intensity until it reaches a threshold (Pierson 2004), when at last it erupts in a dramatic game-changing political event. On this account, realignment occurs because of new subjective issue preferences that transcend party lines. It is these new "crosscutting issues" that slowly undermine pre-existing partisan attachments until at last the process reaches a flashpoint, when do-nothing politicians have no choice but to respond. Thus, Sundquist describes the mounting tension prior to the U.S. presidential election of 1896 in this way: "For twenty years the two-party system had been based on dead issues of the past. It had offered the voters no means of expressing a choice on the crucial issues of domestic economic policy." This process culminated in the Democratic Party's nomination of William Jennings Bryan: "Then suddenly, with the nomination of Bryan in 1896 . . . the day of political unresponsiveness, of evasion and straddling on fundamental burning questions, was over" (Sundquist 1983: 158).

But the critical realignment school is only one perspective. V.O. Key (1959) and Abramson et al. (2010) are, respectively, the original and most recent instantiations of the "secular realignment" perspective, which views realignment as a product of "long-term, or secular, shifts in party attachment among the voters." Key wrote that the gradual "rise and fall of parties may to some degree be the consequence of trends that perhaps persist over decades and elections may mark only steps in a more or less continuous creation of new loyalties and decay of old" (Key 1959: 198). In their series, *Continuity and Change*, Abramson et al. (2010) hold that among the trends that propel the continuous flux of old and new partisan attachments are new issues that divide the electorate in unexpected ways (pp. 6–7). Note that secular realignment does not involve the mounting pressure of crosscutting issues, building to a crescendo, as critical realignment does.

A third perspective, sometimes called the "socialization" perspective, is anchored in a kind of "punctuated equilibrium" model, in which a new issue disrupts old partisan attachments, congeals into new partisan attachments, and then decays until another issue emerges to start the process all over again (Beck 1974; Carmines and Stimson 1989; Carmines et al. 1987; Clubb et al. 1980). Unlike critical realignment, then, in which the long-term build up of a new issue precedes a short-term event that realigns partisan attachments, the punctuated equilibrium model begins with the abrupt appearance of a new issue that grows in salience and eventually trails off. Thus, in their celebrated book, *Issue Evolution*, Carmines and Stimson write, "The model posits that the mass issue evolution begins with a 'critical moment,'" but "the initial increase in mass issue polarization does not complete the process." Rather, "after an extended period of increase, the polarization decays at a gradual pace" (Carmines and Stimson 1989: 143, 157). The issue of black civil rights is an important case in point. That issue burst onto the scene as the Civil Rights Movement gained steam in the 1960s and the parties began to take contrasting positions. For a while thereafter, it remained a source of political division until at last it began its slow decay and economic issues emerged to replace it.

Mayhew's claim that realignment theory has difficulty accounting for events and issues is not particularly convincing in light of the importance of these factors across a range of perspectives. Events and issues work differently in each case to be sure, but they are indispensable mechanisms nonetheless.

*

We conclude as always with the arguments of the book. First, to understand the field, I have insisted that one must understand sociology's contribution to it. If the issue voter is primarily a response to the partisan voter, then it is related to sociology indirectly by lineage. One might say that the issue voter approach may never have arisen, or at least may not have arisen in the way that it did, without Michigan's intervening reaction to Columbia. The chapter does not especially "move the ball down the field" as it were with respect to my argument about the diversity of sociological approaches. It does, however, provide further support for my third claim, which is that a disciplinary turf war would obscure the similarities between sociological and other social scientific approaches to democratic party politics. The issue voter approach has retained the Columbia model's preoccupation with individual vote choice as well as its methodological commitment to individual-level survey data. In fact, as both Rabinowitz and Macdonald (1989) and Carmines and Huckfeldt (1996) point out, spatial theory has become the dominant voter-centered tradition in the field and thus the pre-eminent descendant of the first modern voter studies. My fourth argument has to do with the insularity of voter-centered approaches on the one hand, and party-centered approaches on the other. As we have seen, the historical nemesis of the issue voter is the Michigan model, another voter-centered perspective. Fifth, this approach, like the other approaches thus far, does not contemplate the intersection of party, state, and society. It is mostly agnostic on the state. Downs does suggest that a society with a centrist distribution of voters and a two-party system is the most stable kind of democratic regime, but the state, even in this narrow sense, is present only in the background. It is the moderation of the electorate that is the main determinant of stability, not the practices and institutions of the state itself. Parties, too, are present here, perhaps even more than they are in the previous two chapters, but their interaction with society is rather limited. In classical spatial theory, parties are busy seeking out the median voter. In later variants, parties work to adjust the voters' "perceived policy distance" between them and their rivals. Society thus construed – that is, primarily as the mass electorate –

even separates voters from social movements. On the revisionists' account, for example, the civil rights and Vietnam War protests are important, but they amount to a contextual factor that voters take into account as they make their choices.

Part II

Party-Centered Approaches

4

The Oligarchical Party

The oligarchical party approach consists of three theoretical traditions, each of which suggests that parties serve at the pleasure of an organized minority, even (and perhaps *especially*) under conditions of liberal democracy. Most of the scholars in this chapter are skeptical of romanticized notions of democracy, which insist that parties represent the wishes of the people. The first tradition, which I call "The Iron Rule," and others sometimes called "Elite Theory," holds that the demands of organization under mass suffrage inevitably lead to the separation of party leaders from their constituents. In time, the party becomes mobilized for the sole purpose of keeping its leadership in power (Michels [1911] 1962; Weber [1922] 1968). The Iron Rule is bigger than Michels and Weber, who are its most well-known exponents, however, and I spend some time tracing its lineage through Tocqueville ([1835] 1965), Mosca ([1896] 1939), Pareto ([1901] 1968), Ostrogorski ([1902] 1964), and Sorel ([1908] 1969).

The second tradition is "Power Elite Theory," and is seen by some (e.g., Lipset) as the American descendant or variant of the Iron Rule. Nevertheless, as I seek to demonstrate, it is palpably distinct from the latter. Whereas the Iron Rule presupposes that the party becomes divorced and increasingly autonomous from its base, in power elite theory, the party is infiltrated in various ways (e.g., personnel, campaign contributions) by the rich and powerful. Parties are oligarchical, because the power elite influences and directs their activity (Clawson et al. 1992; Domhoff

1978, 1998; Hunter [1953] 1963; Mills [1956] 1957; Mizruchi 1992).

The third tradition centers on patronage, which is also often referred to as "machine" or "clientelistic" politics. The patronage tradition examines the ways in which parties use economic dependency to maintain social control over their constituents, and in doing so, acquire or retain state power. The so-called "neoclassical" theory of patronage (Banfield and Wilson 1967; Kitschelt and Wilkinson 2007; Scott 1972) holds that social control is maintained through the use of material incentives, whereas an alternative perspective suggests that patronage parties rely on symbolic forms of power (Auyero 2001).

The Iron Rule

Early Influences: Tocqueville, Mosca, Pareto, Ostrogorski, and Sorel

Alexis de Tocqueville's ([1835] 1965) observations in *Democracy in America* are numerous, broad, and thus readily usable for even competing theoretical arguments. In contemporary sociology, he is often taken to argue that liberal democracy requires a robust civil society that can check the overweening power of the state.[1] But that is not the only reading of Tocqueville, and while his inclusion in this chapter will raise some eyebrows, I assure you he is here only because of his influence on Ostrogorski, who, in turn, influenced Weber and Michels (Weber 1946: 104–11; Lipset 1964: xii n7, xiii, xviii).

Among Tocqueville's countless observations, three were particularly influential. First, Tocqueville was critical of parties that were driven exclusively by the private interests of their leadership, preferring instead political organizations that served the *public* interest. Private interests, he conceded, were unavoidable, but the better parties were those whose struggles subordinated such interests to those of the entire people. In this, he did not lament the ability of parties to disrupt society: he would rather that society be turned upside down on matters of real import than stirred by meaningless controversies. Second, in contrast to the voter-centered approaches in the first half of this book, Tocqueville seemed to imply that parties were relatively autonomous from society – otherwise it would not have been possible for parties to convulse the public-at-large. Third, Tocqueville distinguished between ideological or programmatic parties that were committed to abstract ideals, and parties concerned primarily with power for its own sake. However, Tocqueville held that the programmatic parties of the United States were extinct by the 1830s and, significantly, mourned their passing. These claims may be glimpsed in his discussion of "great" and "small" parties.

According to Tocqueville, the struggle between America's "great" parties – the Federalist and Republican – was a struggle between competing principles that concerned the republic as a whole and were therefore fought in the name of the public interest. Tocqueville writes, "The political parties which I style great are those which cling to principles more than to their consequences; to general, and not to special cases; to ideas, and not to men." The principles to which the great parties adhered, he clarifies, were "moral principles of a high order, such as the love of equality and independence." This necessarily inflamed the general public, but the disruption did not appear to bother Tocqueville. Society may be "convulsed" and "torn" by great parties but in doing so, great parties "save it by salutary perturbation" ([1835] 1965: 161–2).

Yet the age of great parties was over by the 1830s when Tocqueville toured the United States. "America," he lamented, "has already lost the great parties which once divided the nation; and if her happiness is considerably increased, her morality has suffered by their extinction." This is because newer parties were animated by lesser questions of private instead of public interest. "The parties by which the Union is menaced," he opines, "do not rest upon abstract principles, but upon temporal interests," which "disturb" the country "to no good end." Temporal interests include, for instance, the debate over the tariff, in which one party championed a duty on foreign imports to protect domestic manufacturing, while the other party schemed to oppose it by mobilizing rural voters. That selfish private interests are the heart and soul of modern parties is clear in his description of how parties are formed:

> A political aspirant in the United States begins by discriminating his own interest, and by calculating upon those interests which may be collected around, and amalgamated with it: he then contrives to discover some doctrine or some principle which may suit the purposes of this new association, and which he adopts in order to forward his party and to secure its popularity ... When these preliminaries are terminated, the new party is ushered into the political world. ([1835] 1965: 161, 164)

The pursuit of calculated gain is therefore according to Tocqueville in the very DNA of any party seeking to compete for office in the United States. From its inception, the "political aspirant" identifies "his own interest" and from there advances a doctrine and builds an entire organization around the realization of that interest.

Though in fact he shares quite a bit in common with Tocqueville, Gaetano Mosca, in his book, *The Ruling Class*, was explicitly dismissive of him, because he witnessed only the earliest stage in the American experiment with democracy (see Mosca [1896] 1939: 152n1). Had Tocqueville seen what became of that experiment, it is possible that he would have reached the same conclusion Mosca had, namely, that universal suffrage was merely a new mechanism for realizing an old aim: the installation of a ruling class. For Mosca, the idea that voters choose their own leaders is a fiction. Representative government, like absolutism, is a political system in which an organized minority imposes its will on an unorganized majority. This is the very definition of oligarchy. He writes,

> When we say that the voters "choose" their representative, we are using a language that is very inexact. The truth is that the representative *has himself elected* by the voters, and, if that phrase should seem too inflexible and too harsh to fit some cases, we might qualify it by saying that *his friends have him elected*. In elections, as in all other manifestations of social life, those who have the will and, especially, the moral, intellectual and material *means* to force their will upon

others take the lead over the others and command them. ([1896] 1939: 154)

While Mosca adds the argument that an organized minority pos-sesses the means to coerce the rest into compliance, his vision of political parties is essentially that of Tocqueville, for party forma-tion is a private affair, executed by the leader and his friends.

Casting more doubt on the notion of "the people's choice," he insists that the mass electorate would be incapable of choosing their representatives without the coordination of their far-flung scattered wills. This is accomplished by presenting a narrow selection of candidates who have some chance of winning, and those who have some chance of winning are generally those who are championed by "*organized minorities*" ([1896] 1939: 154; emphasis in original).

Further, an organized minority projects a narrow set of social values or forces in directing the state; it does not take its marching orders from the putative wants and needs of the public or even of the mass of constituents who voted for their candidate. This is because the organized minorities who champion a candidate form upon "common material interests, on ties of family, class, religion, sect or political party." Thus, for all of the conceits of classical democratic theory, in practice, representative government does not result in government by the majority, but quite the contrary, "the participation of a certain number of social values in the guid-ance of the state" ([1896] 1939: 155).

Closely associated with Mosca's work is Vilfredo Pareto's *The Rise and Fall of the Elites* (Livingstone 1939: xxxvi; Zetterberg 1968: 15–16). Still, Pareto's target is not the optimistic tone of democratic theory as it is for Mosca, but, it seems, the notion that the ascendancy of socialist parties at the turn of the twentieth century represented a new frontier, in which for the first time, the people could at last rule. His summary argument is the doctrine of "the circulation of elites," according to which, "the history of man is the history of the continuous replacement of certain elites: as one ascends, another declines" ([1901] 1968: 36). Pareto makes this claim without exception, not even excepting the socialist party.

The decline of the old elite occurs largely because of a twin movement. The first is the softening of the old elite. Humanitarian sentiment, Pareto says, sets in among their number, such that for example, they begin to feel guilty and scandalized by the precarious living and working conditions of the poor. This leads to a corresponding decline in their ability or willingness to defend their position by force, for if capitalists or "the bourgeoisie" are sympathetic to their employees' plight, then they are less likely to crush the working class as it grows in power. Importantly, and this is the second tendency, as the softness of the old elite sets in, the greed of the old elite continues unabated. Thus, he observes that the old elite "does not lose its rapacity and greed for the goods of others, but rather tends as much as possible to increase its unlawful appropriations and to indulge in major usurpations of the national patrimony." The elite, of their own doing, introduces a dangerous vulnerability to their rule: "on one hand it makes the yoke heavier, and on the other it has less strength to maintain it" ([1901] 1968: 59). As evidence of the softening of the old elite, Pareto points out that the leaders of socialist parties have "almost without exception been bourgeois; that is, they hail from the ranks of the old aristocracy." The bourgeoisie has behaved so shamefully, he says, that its "better part" has jumped ship, thereby "weakening the dominant class still more, so that it becomes impoverished and loses its strongest, most moral, and honest men" ([1901] 1968: 73).

A different dual movement signals the rise of the new elite. At first, the latter, whether bourgeois or socialist, justifies its rise using altruistic rhetoric. That the elite stands for particular interests, especially its leadership, is never admitted. Publicly they suggest that they will stand up for the good of the many, for the entire citizenry, for the republic. But like any elite, Pareto cautions, the new elite is invariably oligarchical, even the socialists, and this becomes no clearer than when they at last rise to power:

> Of course, once victory is won, it subjugates the erstwhile allies, or, at best, offers them some formal concessions. Such is the history of the struggles fought by the *plebs* and *patres* in Rome; such is the history

of the victory which the bourgeoisie won over the nobility of feudal origin, a victory well noted by modern socialists. ([1901] 1968]: 36)

Accordingly, of the would-be representatives of the working class, he writes, "It is an illusion to believe that it is the people who stand at the head of the dominant class today. Those who stand there . . . are part of a new and future elite which leans upon the people." Indeed, he points to already existing friction between the socialist leadership and their rank-and-file, a sign that "with the passing of time" the socialists will resemble what in Rome was "the contrast between the aristocracy of the *plebs* and the others" ([1901] 1968: 72).

Like Mosca and Pareto, Moisei Ostrogorski was skeptical of the notion that the political elite cared at all about the great mass of the people, but unlike the preceding two authors, he theorized the duplicity of the elite, with Tocqueville, as the product of self-interested political parties. In a famous passage from his book *Democracy and the Organization of Parties*, he writes, "As soon as a party, were it created for the noblest object, perpetuates itself, it tends inevitably toward power, and as soon as it makes that its end, its master passion is to maintain itself against all opposition, with no scruple as to the means" ([1902] 1964: 355). Ostrogorski thus introduces a soon-to-be influential distinction between the founding motives of the party and the obsession with power that takes hold as it struggles to stay alive. Ostrogorski's oligarchical party therefore possesses a means-end rationality. In the above passage, "power" is the party's "end," and the "means" to that end are employed with "no scruple" as its "master passion" is to "maintain" and "perpetuate" itself. The party is a relentlessly vote-maximizing individual *incarnated* in the form of an organization. In this, the well-known influence of Tocqueville on Ostrogorski's own approach to party and society becomes clear.

Echoing the Tocquevillian claim that American parties originate with the self-interest of political aspirants, Ostrogorski argued that the birth of British and American parties may be traced to the rise of individualism and the challenge it posed to the once absolute power of the monarchy and aristocratic ruling class. The story of party formation begins with "the idea which presided over its birth, which viewed the object of democracy – the greatest happiness of the greatest number – in a narrowly individualist way, by placing it wholly in the abstract and self-sufficing individual." Put simply, the advocates of modern democracy believed that the surest way to achieve the greatest happiness for the greatest number of people was to protect the right of *individuals* to pursue their wants freely. Having established democracy in Britain and America, however, the people now required "representative institutions" like Parliament that could act as "the means of ensuring the security of their persons and property." It then developed "extra-legal" organizations – parties – "in order to assert emphatically the power of the autonomous individual." But in doing so, the people established a democracy that "appeared to live only for electioneering," and in which "the task of government was identified with electoral operations." Consequently, "from a means" of preserving the power of the autonomous individual, "election became an end." The pursuit of individual self-interest had, in other words, transmuted itself into the party's pursuit of political power with paradoxical results, for this transformation subordinated the will of the people to the will of the party. It "placed the real power in the hands of the election agencies and their managers, who, on pretence of helping bewildered public opinion, thus became its masters" ([1902] 1964: 322–3).

As in Tocqueville, then, Ostrogorski suggests that the "self-sufficing individual" is in the party's genetic code. If political parties pursue power without regard to scruples, it is because they were founded to preserve the individual right to satisfy their own wants without interference from the monarch. The party, in other words, institutionalized means-end rationality and then subsequently disempowered the self-interested individuals it once promised to protect.

A final early influence on what would become the "iron rule of oligarchy" is Georges Sorel's ([1908] 1969) book, *The Illusions of Progress*. With Pareto, Sorel shared a suspicion of the socialist claim that their party, above all others, represented "progress" in the sense that the interests of more people than ever before would be represented in the halls of government. In response to this claim, Sorel argues that the very idea of progress, which originates in the time of the absolutist *ancien régime* of Louis XIV in France, is an ideology – a justification for the rule of the dominant class even under conditions of democracy. He writes, "All ideas related to progress combine together in an extraordinary and sometimes ridiculous way, because democracy has very few ideas it can properly call its own and because it lives almost entirely on the heritage of the *ancien régime*" ([1908] 1969: 152).

To get to this conclusion, Sorel's argument takes roughly four steps. He begins with a genealogy of the idea of progress as a philosophy of history, in which human civilization is said to be on a linear timeline toward perfection. Second, this philosophy of history is said to have originated under absolutism when the nobility justified their rule by suggesting that they were society's only hope for progress. Each succeeding dominant class then used the idea of progress to justify their own rule. Thirdly, Sorel insists that the idea of progress is a smokescreen for the fact that control of the modern state is simply being passed from one elite to another. Moreover, with each new elite, the state has grown stronger and ever more dominant. The final step in Sorel's argument is that non-elites have correspondingly become ever more passive ([1908] 1969: 152).

The Iron Rule

Having traced the antecedents of the Iron Rule, we turn now to Max Weber, the elder statesman in Robert Michels' academic circle. It might be useful at this point to begin with a few definitions. A modern party for Weber cannot preside over a one-party state. Weber would not have considered the Syrian Ba'ath Party, for instance, a party. "The modern type of party," he holds, "does not arise except in the legal state with a representative constitution." Additionally, when the state can only be legally administered by a certain party as is typically the case in one-party states, Weber argues that "it ceases to be a party" ([1922] 1968: 287). To the extent that parties meet these conditions, they are "modern parties," of which there are two types, echoing Tocqueville's distinction of "small" and "great" parties. There are "patronage parties," which are "solely concerned with the attainment of power for their leaders and with securing positions in the administrative staff for their own members" ([1922] 1968: 285). There are also "ideological parties," which "predominantly and consciously act in the interests of a status group or a class or of certain objective policies or of abstract principles" ([1922] 1968: 285).[2] Simply put, there are some parties that seek power for its own sake, and others that seek power for more idealistic reasons. But for Weber, both types of parties are intrinsically oligarchical, because they are bureaucratic organizations.

The logic of bureaucratization distances the party from the people for two reasons. First, bureaucracies operate through hierarchy and specialization. Accordingly, parties are run primarily by "party leaders and their staffs," whereas "active party members" simply fall in behind the leadership, and "the inactive masses of electors or voters are merely objects whose votes are sought at election time" ([1922] 1968: 285). This is true of all the key party functions. For example, with respect to nominating the party's candidates, Weber writes, "The designation of these candidates takes place within the parties, for it stands to reason that party leaders and their followers, not the amorphous activities of voters, organize the contest for votes" ([1922] 1968: 1129). Nor do the people have input in writing the party platform. "Even in mass parties with very democratic constitutions," he observes, "the voters and most of the rank and file members do not (or do only formally) participate in the drafting of the program" ([1922] 1968: 1396).

Second, because hierarchy and specialization require the filling of staff positions (e.g., assistant press secretary), political appointments (e.g., postmaster, minister of foreign affairs), and elected offices (e.g., councilperson, Member of Parliament), bureaucratization generates the currency with which to both buy off potential challengers and make existing party loyalists economically dependent on the party. Thus, Weber makes frequent references to "the material interests of the job hunters" ([1922] 1968: 1132) and a "salaried officialdom" ([1922] 1968: 1396). Economic interests and political ambitions in turn reinforce and expand the party's reliance on bureaucratic specialization, thereby generating a kind of recursive loop: "The more bureaucratization advances and the more substantial the interests in benefices and other opportunities become, the more surely does the party organization fall into the hands of experts" ([1922] 1968: 1131).

The paradox of modern democracy, then, is that because electoral competition is conducted through parties, the people have very little influence on the political process.

Weber in fact characterizes party organization as "frequently strict and 'authoritarian'" ([1922] 1968: 939). For this reason he implies that democracy is really a misnomer, for "The *demos* itself, in the sense of a shapeless mass, never 'governs' larger associations, but rather is governed" ([1922] 1968: 984–5).[3]

Weber's protégé and colleague, Robert Michels, advanced a similar analysis of party domination but emphasized the demands of political struggle in necessitating the turn to organization. A sociologist and former socialist activist, Michels sought to make sense of the antidemocratic tendencies of his erstwhile party, the German Social Democratic Party (SPD), then the largest socialist party in the world. Why did progressive parties tend to oligarchy, and why then was democracy itself a lost cause ([1911] 1962: 7, 50–1)?

The answer may be found in Michels' definition of the modern political party, namely, "the methodical organization of the electoral masses" ([1911] 1962: 334). In order to win the support of a majority of voters, workers, who are "defenseless in the hands of those who are economically stronger," have no choice but to unite collectively in unions and parties, for the "importance and influence of the working class are directly proportional to its numerical strength" ([1911] 1962: 61–2). Accordingly, workers establish hierarchical bureaucracies, consisting of specialized delegations, committees, and a staff of party operatives. The irony is that in doing what they must do to defeat the ruling class, workers pay a great price: the logic of organization works in such a way that the party's leading experts are elevated to positions far removed from the workers whom they ostensibly represent. He writes, "The technical specialization that inevitably results from all extensive organization renders necessary what is called expert leadership . . . Thus, the leaders, who were at first no more than the executive organs of the collective will, soon emancipate themselves from the mass and become independent of its control. Organization implies the tendency to oligarchy" ([1911] 1962: 70).

Lower-level party operatives, who often mobilize voters at the ward and precinct levels, are perhaps in the best position to check the oligarchical tendencies of the party by virtue of their close proximity to regular voters and their knowledge of the scandalous inner workings of the party leadership. Indeed, Michels acknowledges that some party workers "carry on a difficult internal struggle against their own skepticism." However, Michels adds that their economic dependence on party success keeps them in check: "For those who have been thus disillusioned, no backward path is open," he writes, "They are enchained by their own past. They have a family, and this family must be fed" ([1911] 1962: 208).

But the demands of electoral mobilization are not the only aspect of political struggle that breed hierarchical party organizations. Parties organize in order to seamlessly assume the levers of state power in the event of an electoral victory. Thus, the manager of a successful electoral campaign often becomes the newly elected official's chief of staff, while the campaign spokesperson transitions into the role of press secretary. In parliamentary democracies, the official opposition party assembles a "shadow cabinet" not only to hector the government's actual cabinet, but also to practice for the day when the opposition takes power. Michels was particularly rueful of this phenomenon, because of his once ardent commitment to socialist revolution. Originally a party mobilized to destroy the capitalist state, the SPD became instead, "a party which, organized itself like a government on the small scale, hopes some day to assume the reins of government upon the large scale. The revolutionary political party is a state within a state" ([1911] 1962: 335).

For Michels, democracy is therefore nothing more than a system in which the opposition merely aims "at the substitution of one clique of the dominant classes for another." It amounts to the reproduction of what Mosca called "the ruling class" and what Pareto called "the circulation of elites" ([1911] 1962: 343). In this way, the party of the common man becomes no better than the party of the elite that it seeks to defeat. The passage that is often referred to as Michels' "iron law of oligarchy" underscores this central point:

> Reduced to its most concise expression, the fundamental sociological law of political parties . . . may be formulated in the following terms: "It is organization which gives birth to the dominion of the elected over electors, of the mandataries over the mandators, of the delegates over the delegators. Who says organization, says oligarchy." ([1911] 1962: 365)

Power Elite Theory

The next tradition in the oligarchical party approach is sometimes seen as the American variant of Michels' work. Its earliest practitioners were C. Wright Mills ([1956] 1957) and Floyd Hunter ([1953] 1963). Mills' argument in his classic study of *The Power Elite* is that "political outsiders," who are members of the corporate rich and the military establishment, have increasingly infiltrated parties and the state, which were once the sole preserve of career politicians and civil servants. He emphasizes, "Neither professional party politicians, nor professional bureaucrats are now at the executive centers of decision." Party is oligarchical, not in the Michelsian sense, where the mechanism of organization transforms the party of the working class into a conservative force, but in the conspiratorial sense that party is merely a *vehicle* of the rich and well-placed to consolidate their power. Mills describes the ascendancy of political outsiders or the "political directorate" as a virtual *coup d'état*. Referring to the Eisenhower administration (1953–1961), for example, Mills writes, "This administration, in fact, is largely an inner circle of political outsiders who have taken over the key executive posts of administrative command; it is composed of members and agents of the corporate rich and of the high military in an uneasy alliance with selected professional party politicians" ([1956] 1957: 231, 241).

Thus, while Lipset would argue that Mills was a late follower of Michels' thesis (Lipset 1962: 36), in fact, Mills is distinct from the latter in significant ways. First, unlike Michels who views the corruption of the SPD as evidence of the circulation of successive elite groups, Mills speaks of one coherent social class and suggests that the party becomes merely a specialized appendage of this class. Thus, he adds that the "executive centers of decision" are "occupied by the political directorate of the power elite" ([1956] 1957: 241). Second, Mills rejects the notion that party remains independent of powerful social groups like the corporate rich. This is at variance with the previous tradition, which presupposes the autonomy of party from society. In Michels, for example, workers organize a party to set their superior numbers against the economic might of their bosses, but the demands of organization distance the emerging party leadership until they are wholly independent and aloof from the masses from which they sprung. The SPD is oligarchical precisely because its working-class base is disconnected from the party that is supposed to represent it. By contrast, for Mills, the party is oligarchical because the power elite, which is *already* disconnected from the masses, has taken it over. A social group has, in other words, infiltrated the once exclusive sphere of the politician and civil servant and kicked them out.

Floyd Hunter's (1953) book, *Community Power Structure*, is a pioneering work on "director interlocks," a term which refers to the fact that corporate executives sit not only on each others' boards of directors, but also on government committees. Like the other authors in this chapter, Hunter suggests that "This situation does not square with the concepts of democracy we have been taught to revere" ([1953] 1963: 1).

Hunter is most interested in theorizing "community power." In this, his overarching hypothesis is that such power operates through relationships, such that the power of any given individual must be "structured into associational, clique, or institutional patterns to be effective" ([1953] 1963: 6). It is not enough to assert that business leaders control civic affairs; one must also expose the relationships that enable power to flow. In this case, the power of business leaders is enacted through director interlocks, which he uncovers by conducting interviews with local actors in "Regional City." The "cliques" that result from director interlocks are organized roughly by industry (e.g., banking, utilities, etc.) and provide the key decision makers in civic affairs ([1953] 1963: 77–8). This is accomplished through a kind of delegate system, whereby each clique sends representatives to policy-making bodies that approve important measures. Note that Hunter's argument proceeds in two steps. First, the elite associate socially with one another both in sub-groups called cliques and in a larger umbrella group of cliques. Second, businessmen run the political apparatus of the city through this network of relationships. He writes, "The pattern of business dominance of civic affairs in Regional City is a fact. No other institution is as dominant in community life as the economic institution." Business leaders, he finds, "are related to one another as directors of boards of corporate enterprises in Regional City." This is meant to show that "the economic interests of the leaders are in some measure coordinate" ([1953] 1963: 76). Finally, he adds in reference to the activity of "cliques" or "crowds" in matters of policy, "representatives from each crowd are drawn into any discussion relative to a major community decision" ([1953] 1963: 78).

The work of Mills and Hunter set off a reaction among political scientists called "pluralists," who bristled at the implication that the United States was not a democracy (see pp. 114–16). Their objections were many, but they amounted to one key claim: while there is indeed an elite, that elite is divided by party, social relationships, and economic competition, among other cleavages. Later, when the next generation of sociologists would confirm Hunter's preliminary findings by documenting the ubiquity of director interlocks (thereby demonstrating that the elite was unified), the pluralists would insist that sociologists had yet to prove that this unified elite overrules the objections of non-elites. In the absence of overt conflict, they held, we can only assume that non-elites are satisfied with elite rule and are therefore not subjugated. In any case, the pluralists added, elites no longer run their own companies; control has passed to their managers. The following three sociologists – Domhoff, Mizruchi, and Clawson et al. – offered critical rejoinders to these objections.[4] I cite these and not the many others who figured prominently in this debate, because their findings bear directly on party politics.

In his contemporary classic *Who Really Rules?*, G. William Domhoff (1978) demonstrated that elites were in fact one unified social group, but Domhoff's later work is more important for the study of party politics. It shows both that there is a coherent elite in the United States and that this elite has infiltrated the democratic process. Indeed, for Domhoff the latter claim is at the core of the Millsian tradition: "If there is anything to a power-elite analysis of the United States," he writes, "it is in its ability to show how the power elite operates within – not outside – the democratic process" (1998: 201–2). That said, Domhoff diverges from Mills in a few ways. The military establishment more or less drops out of his analysis, so that the emphasis centers on the corporate rich. In addition, to the extent that the rich infiltrate the political process, they do so not just by surreptitiously placing their agents in key positions, but also by contributing money to both major parties.

Accordingly, much of his data turn on the dynamics of campaign finance and candidate background. With respect to campaign finance, his aim is to demonstrate that corporate contributions to America's major parties dwarf the contributions of labor and other groups. For example, he notes, "a study of campaign finance for 1994 estimated that total corporate contributions were $289 million compared to $42 million from organized labor, a ratio of 6.9 to 1." Domhoff adds that ever since restrictions on campaign finance were lifted in 1979,[5] the corporate rich have contributed the lion's share of "soft money," which is designated for the mysterious practice of "party building." He observes, "In 1996, 92 percent of soft money came from business leaders and their corporations, 5 percent from organized labor, and 3 percent from other sources." In addition, the wealthy are shown to hedge their bets by contributing to, and thus controlling, both major parties. According to the aforementioned 1994 study, "corporate PACs gave a total of $131 million in 1994 – $67 million to the Democrats, $64 million to the Republicans" (1998: 218, 221).

The entrenchment of corporate interests in partisan politics is further secured by virtue of the background of candidates and elected representatives. "Politicians," he notes, "are from the top 10–15 percent of the occupational and income ladders" and "a great many elected officials in the United States are lawyers. In 1996, for example 53 percent of the senators and 40 percent of the representatives were lawyers." Further, although American presidents tend to stress their humble beginnings, very few presidents as it turns out "have been from outside the very wealthiest circles." Examples of wealthy commanders-in-chief include Theodore Roosevelt, William H. Taft, Franklin D. Roosevelt, John F. Kennedy, and George H.W. Bush. The same might be said of members of the legislative branch. Citing a journalist who examined income disclosure forms in 1994, Domhoff points out that "at least twenty-eight members of the Senate and fifty members of the House were millionaires" (1998: 226, 232).

In *The Structure of Corporate Political Action*, Mark Mizruchi uses data on campaign contributions in a different way. Mizruchi begins by suggesting that the question of whether elites are unified or divided is a false choice. Of course there is conflict, he says, but elites *do* unite as a class albeit in ways not previously understood. First, elites engage in collective action, not interpersonally, but interorganizationally. That is, a Rockefeller does not talk to a Vanderbilt, who then talks to a Carnegie to get political parties to squash pro-labor legislation. Instead, *firms* talk to each other, frequently through their managers. Second, elites do not unify in all cases; they do so on two conditions. One is "interfirm relations." This means that firms unify when they are obstacles to one another: if one firm has the power to coerce the other out of the market, it will use director interlocks (i.e., invite someone from the competing firm to join their board of directors) to get the potential nemesis on their team. Another is "similarity of structural position": this means that the firms are in the same primary industry or are headquartered in the same town (1992: 12). Contrary to the pluralist claim that elites are divided by economic competition, then, Mizruchi argues that competition actually promotes class unity in collective action.

How then does he prove that these are the conditions of business unity? Mizruchi demonstrates that when competing firms meet these two conditions, their "political action committees" or "PACs" tend to donate to similar candidates and parties. When they do not meet these conditions, firms tend to make conflicting donations. The same is true for testimony before the U.S. Congress. When corporations are in the same primary industry and are fierce competitors with one another, they tend to testify with each other for or against the same thing (1992: 123). In short, elites do work together to infiltrate the political process, but collective action is conditional on structural factors.

Clawson et al.'s (1992) book, *Money Talks*, is also in the power elite tradition but draws mainly from interviews with PAC officers from the largest corporate PACs in the United States. It is this added level of access that gives us further perspective on the infiltration of parties by the corporate elite. If in Mizruchi we find that economic competition does not divide the elite (but rather unifies them), then in Clawson et al. we see that partisan allegiance does not fracture the elite either. With the exception of Senator Howard Metzenbaum (an Ohio Democrat) and the possible exception of Senator Ted Kennedy, they find that "Essentially *all* members of Congress," regardless of party, "are at least potentially willing to help out, to give them access, to let them make their case" (1992: 114–15). That American politicians must take tough stands against big business is apparently no concern. There is an unspoken understanding that a member will have to vote one way in public to survive politically in their district or state (e.g., in favor of environmental protections), but that same member may achieve concessions and otherwise compromise the bill in committee before it even comes up for a vote. As one PAC officer put it, "We are not big on voting records . . . Probably what's more important is what's thrashed out internally in some of the important committees in Congress" (1992: 118).

Their research also tends to confirm Mizruchi's findings and cast doubt on the pluralist assertion that business is divided by countless cleavages (e.g., small vs. big; region vs. region; competitors in the same industry; industry vs. industry, etc.), so that while their potential power is high, their actual impact on the political process is low. Clawson et al.'s analysis of donations made by all large PACs revealed that if there is any split at all it is between "a unified business-Republican group on one side and a labor-women-environmentalist-Democratic group on the other." Another analysis of theirs, this time of corporate PACs alone, showed that "In about three out of four races business can be classified as unified, giving at least nine times as much to one candidate as to the other" (1992: 160). They add that competitors in the same industry are most likely to work together. One PAC officer says of a competitor of his, "We hate each other, but I have a very good relationship with them down here, and often we work together on the Hill for certain bills. The [provision] in Z bill was something we worked on together because it benefits us even though in that business they have more of a share than we do" (1992: 173).

Patronage: Machine Politics and Clientelism

If Clawson et al. emphasize economic dependency on corporate PACs, then the last tradition in this chapter stresses economic dependency on party resources. Recall that for both Weber and Michels, the oligarchical party maintains control of the government in part through material incentives to party voters and workers, such that any deviation in loyalty results in the automatic shut-off of partisan largesse. The patronage tradition is devoted precisely to this relationship.

Machine Politics

According to Banfield and Wilson's *City Politics*, the foundational study in this tradition, a party machine is a political organization that maintains control of government, usually at the local level, through a system of patronage, whereby party workers (e.g., precinct captains, ward leaders) confer benefits (e.g., jobs, favors) on individuals in exchange for votes or influence among a community of voters. For example, precinct captains may get votes in a neighborhood with "gravy" or favors such as a holiday turkey or a municipal job. Party workers, in turn, are recruited with still other gravy like higher paid "no show" jobs that do not require the employee to do anything but receive a paycheck (Banfield and Wilson 1967: 119).

Banfield and Wilson emphasize that the party machine, like a business, uses incentives to maintain control over their base, and thereby the reins of government. They write, "Business organizations are machines in that they rely largely upon specific, material incentives (such as salaries) to secure dependable, close control over their employees. A political machine is a business organization in a particular field of business – getting votes and winning elections" (1967: 115). Note that principle and ideology are irrelevant or comprise at best an occasional nuisance in the world of machine politics. For Banfield and Wilson, this "political indifferentism" is intrinsic to the party machine. "The machine, therefore, is apolitical," they write, "it is interested only in making and distributing income – mainly money – to those who run it and work for it. Political principle is foreign to it, and represents a danger and a threat to it" (1967: 116).

Although Banfield and Wilson insist that the machine itself is a purely self-serving organization, they also argue, quite famously, that the influence of machine politics varies with the class and ethnic groups that prevail in a given community. Because machines flourish when they can use material and nonmaterial inducements to deliver votes, the Anglo-Saxon "public-regarding" ethos, which elevates the public good over private interests, undermines the lifeblood of the machine. As a rule, machines tend to have influence in new immigrant working-class cities and wards, where the voters have a "private-regarding" ethos and where such inducements tend to help struggling families. Thus, Banfield and Wilson hold that "The Anglo-Saxon Protestant middle-class style of politics, with its emphasis upon the obligation of the individual to participate in public affairs and to seek the good of the community 'as a whole' (which implies, among other things, the necessity of honesty, impartiality, and efficiency) was fundamentally incompatible with the immigrants' style of politics, which took no account of community" (1967: 41, 123) The "immigrant ethos," by contrast, is held by those "who identify with the ward or neighborhood rather than the city 'as a whole' . . . and who are far less interested in the efficiency, impartiality, and honesty of local government than in its readiness to confer material benefits of one sort or another upon them" (1967: 46). In this, Banfield and Wilson suggest that "society" is not wholly passive in the face of the party machine. Indeed, whether or not a machine will take hold in a given community depends crucially on the demographic makeup and the putative "ethos" of the people.

Clientelism

A very similar literature on patronage is the scholarship on "clientelism," which refers to the dependency of the client on her or his "patron," who is often a party official. The distinction between machine politics and clientelism is unclear, as both approaches in substance tend to assume that parties use material incentives to maintain control over their constituency and the state. Nevertheless, the two concepts tend to be employed in different contexts: clientelism is used to describe patronage in the developing world, often in rural contexts, whereas the party machine tends to denote a bygone or disappearing form of urban politics in the developed world.[6]

A classic study of clientelism is Scott's (1972) *Comparative Political Corruption*. Parties, especially in societies undergoing the transition to democratic suffrage, all confront a similar organizing problem: how to gain the support of large numbers of people when violence is at least formally prohibited and when there is no other mechanism for ensuring social control. Material interest, he says, is a convenient solution to this problem:

> Few viable political bonds except those of material self-interest are available to build a large political party among poor, heterogeneous,

transitional populations. Self-interest thus provides the necessary political cement. (1972: 118)

If impoverished clients receive favors that improve their quality of life, then on the other end, parties gain a political base, which, depending on its size, may give them greater access to resources for themselves and their clients. In addition, patronage ensures a cadre of loyal party operatives, who can do the grunt work of distributing favors to voters on the ground and mobilizing support for the party leadership at election time. Parties engage in clientelistic practices, then, because it is a convenient and theoretically non-violent way of inculcating discipline (1972: 119).

Like Banfield and Wilson, though, parties do not give favors in a cultural vacuum. Because they need and want state power, politicians will offer incentives to voters that speak to the specific values of a given community of clients. "Given the pressure to gain support," Scott writes, "a party will emphasize those inducements that are appropriate to the loyalty patterns among its clientele." Thus, parties will offer "protection" to a community, whose loyalty is based on "traditional deference" to their superiors, but then offer "cash payments" to communities with an "individual, family, or small group orientation" (1972: 110). Moreover, parties tend not to appeal to voters from all walks of life, but rather privilege certain ethnic groups at the expense of others, apparently for no other reason than fealty to the patron. In the case of mid-twentieth-century Malaysia, the governing Alliance Party directed the benefits of rural development programs to Malays (as opposed, say, to ethnic Chinese) "who were deemed assets to the party," while "the few areas of solid opposition strength naturally received little or nothing" (1972: 122).

A recent volume edited by Kitschelt and Wilkinson (2007) picks up an important thread of Scott's work, namely, the relationship or "linkage" between party and society in the new democracies of Latin America, the former Soviet bloc, South and Southeast Asia, and Africa. Kitschelt and Wilkinson argue that these new cases challenge our existing theoretical assumptions in two ways.

First, social scientists tend to assume that the relationship between party and society follows the "responsible party government model," according to which (a) voters have certain policy preferences; (b) parties bundle their positions on the issues into party "programs" that they promise to enact if they win; and (c) voters pick the party whose program is most compatible with their policy preferences and then hold the parties accountable to their promises at the next election. The responsible party government model, Kitschelt and Wilkinson contend, ignores the fact that "a quite different type of *patronage-based, party-voter linkage* exists in many countries" where the relationship is not about "democratic" accountability but rather *"clientelistic accountability,"* which *"represents a transaction, the direct exchange of a citizen's vote in return for direct payments or continuing access to employment, goods, and services"* (2007: 2; emphasis in original).

Second, to the extent that scholars have paid any attention at all to clientelistic accountability, they have tended to see it as an extinct form of early western politics, yet Kitschelt and his colleagues find that clientelism has remained "resilient in established party systems in advanced industrial democracies such as Italy, Japan, Austria, and Belgium" (2007: 3). The relationship between parties and voters is therefore ensured not only in an ideological commitment to certain policies and programs (that is, in so-called "programmatic" party politics), but also in a calculated *quid pro quo*.

The Institutionalist Critique

An important figure in the patronage literature, Martin Shefter is a vocal critic of its early works. Shefter ([1977] 1994) refers to Banfield and Wilson's study as one among several examples of the "neoclassical theory of patronage," because it views the party as a business firm, a basic unit of analysis in neoclassical economics. The latter, Shefter observes, is anchored in three assumptions. First, just as firms are assumed to respond to the tastes and preferences of consumers, parties are likewise said to respond to the tastes and preferences of voters. Additionally, the preference of voters for or against patronage depends on voters' social background and cultural heritage, another familiar assumption in neoclassical consumer studies. Finally, because parties are interested in acquiring or remaining in power, they will do what tends to fit with a given community of voters. They will exchange favors for votes if the electorate is composed mainly of immigrants and uprooted peasants who supposedly have a taste for patronage and, in contrast, make policy-oriented promises of collective benefit to the entire community if the electorate is composed mainly of native-born middle-class voters, who are generally hostile to patronage politics (Shefter [1977] 1994: 22–3).

Shefter identifies two problems with neoclassical theory. One is empirical. There are several examples of parties that appeal to the electorate with promises of collective benefit, but whose base is among immigrants and uprooted peasants. These include the Communist Party in Italy and the Socialist Party in Spain. Conversely, there are patronage parties whose main electoral support is among the middle classes. The Christian Democratic Party in Italy and the Radical Party in France are good examples. Another problem is that the neoclassical approach is ahistorical. That is, if a group of voters respond to policy-oriented appeals, it is not because they are of a particular social class and therefore culturally predisposed to like policy, but because parties initially mobilized those voters into their organizations by making such appeals and by encouraging the establishment of powerful grassroots organizations oriented to questions of policy. In this way, Shefter points out that parties do not exactly take the patronage or policy road because of a calculation that one or the other will secure more votes; rather, they do so because of a founding moment or "critical experience" in the institutional history of a party (Shefter [1977] 1994: 23, 29–30).

Amy Bridges ([1984] 1987), in a well-known study of the founding of New York machine politics, is equally suspicious of the argument that "the machine was . . . a product of immigrant culture and ethnic conflict." The approach is problematic for several reasons, she says. City politics were not all or even mainly about ethnic issues or divisions. Additionally, the so-called "party boss" and machine predated a strong immigrant presence in American cities. Lastly, few people actually *wanted* the form of machine politics that took hold in New York City, suggesting that the reason machine politics came to dominate urban electoral competition in the United States had to do with historical factors such as the timing of industrialization and worker suffrage ([1984] 1987: 4–5).

A Symbolic Interpretation of Patronage

Javier Auyero's (2001) work on the Peronist Party in Argentina also challenges the core assumptions of neoclassical theory, but emphasizes cultural as opposed to historical institutionalist factors. Favors do circulate in one direction from the party to the voters, and votes and other forms of political support then sometimes circulate in the other direction from the voters to the party. To assume, however, that the favors themselves are the motive force behind clientelism is to commit an error in two senses. First, it substitutes the scholar's theories ("the scholastic point of view") for the experience of the party brokers and "clients" who actually enact this so-called exchange. Second, the fact that favors precede votes in time does not rule out the possibility either that another factor enables the exchange to take place or that the exchange is dramatizing something else more important (2001: 13, 23).

Like the preceding authors, Auyero views clientelism as a system of domination. Indeed, he writes, "With each problem that they solve for the client, brokers are continually better positioning themselves so that, at election time, they will essentially be able to blackmail their clients, the implied threat being that, if the broker and his or her patron are forced from office, the broker's clients will no longer receive the benefits of social programs established by the patron and run by the broker." Still, such "blackmail" is not enacted so nakedly, but is instead "embedded in a system of representation that masks its true nature," and in doing so enables domination to persist (2001: 123).

Thus, Peronist operatives in Villa Paraíso, a shantytown in metropolitan Buenos Aires, do not merely hand out bags of food, medicines, and steady municipal jobs; they also "perform Evita," the wife of General Peron, who, so the legend goes, gave of herself entirely to alleviate the plight of the poor. Female party brokers in particular enact a gendered "script," in which they telegraph that their work is not a job, but a vocation. An exhausting and all-consuming sacrifice, they recuperate and re-invent Evita by playing the role of "mother to the poor" (2001: 127).

Correspondingly, the clients do not view the favors from party brokers as an exchange, nor do they understand their votes or support at political rallies as obligations. Instead, they view their activities on behalf of the party as acts of either "gratitude" or "collaboration." These themes along with the denial of the exchange itself, Auyero argues, reflect the informal networks and problem-solving strategies that the poor use to survive mass unemployment under neoliberalism. He adds, however, that not all people buy into the performance: those who are distant from the party's immediate ambit (e.g., people who work but do not live in the shantytown) view these exchanges as corruption and manipulation pure and simple, whereas those who are close to the party's inner circle tend to internalize and articulate the symbolic tropes of Peronism (2001: 154–9). The patron–client exchange, to the extent it exists at an abstract level, is therefore enabled and perpetuated by something that is neither rational nor exchange-oriented, namely, the play of symbols that links party brokers to voters.

*

This chapter, along with the other chapters in part II of this book, is a star player in my arguments about the field. To repeat, my first two claims are that to understand this area of inquiry, one must understand the role that sociology plays in its central debates, and to do that one must give up the caricature of sociology as reducible to the Columbia model. With respect to the first argument, the omission of Michels and Weber throughout so much of the literature on vote choice is in my view an unpardonable oversight. The Iron Rule was, and remains to this day, among the most well-known and coherent traditions in the study of democratic party politics. It also preceded the postwar voter studies by at least a generation and is unlikely to have escaped the attention of their authors, yet the debate among the social, partisan, and issue voter approaches proceeded as if the Iron Rule had never existed. With respect to the second argument, I think it is safe to say that the sociologists in this chapter bear little resemblance to those in chapter 1. If the Columbia studies were voter-centered, then the theories in this chapter focus on parties, whether as oligarchical organizations or as infiltrated by the rich and powerful.

Third, the differences between chapters 1 and 4 notwithstanding, I have argued that the competing approaches featured in this book share much in common and that a disciplinary turf war would muddle rather than clarify our sense of where we have been and where we must go next. In a recent review essay, Mudge and Chen (2013) correctly point out that concern for the dynamics of party organization and the latter's relationship with the state and civil society essentially dropped out of the postwar debates. This means that social scientists of all stripes, including sociologists, participated in relegating the oligarchical approach to the dustbin of history. I would add that the narrowing of the field to the determinants of individual vote choice was hardly necessary. For example, Converse's work on the lack of ideological constraint in the mass electorate does not preclude an analysis of oligarchical parties (see pp. 40–1). Under the Iron Rule, parties are more concerned with protecting leaders and preserving state power than with communicating meaningfully with their constituents. If anything, such an analysis would complement the Michigan model's emphasis on the ideological disconnect between parties and voters.

This leads seamlessly into my fourth argument about the isolation of party-centered approaches from their voter-centered counterparts. The oligarchical approach is silent on matters of vote choice, except to say, in the manner of the early patronage tradition, that voters trade their ballots for favors. Conversely, patronage is nowhere in evidence in voter-centered approaches: the main motivations as we have seen are social group loyalty, familial party ID, and issue preferences. Further, the main targets of the oligarchical approach are other party-centered studies that betray some faith in liberal democracy and the salutary influences of parties, especially Left or socialist parties. Here it must be stressed that the scholars in this chapter are not only dissatisfied with the pluralists of chapter 5 below (see pp. 114–16). The Iron Rule and power elite traditions are broadly at variance with the Marxist tradition in chapter 6, which views Left parties as the best hope for the emancipation of the working class (see pp. 137–53). Indeed, the main thrust of the Michelsian critique is that the demands of organization paradoxically distance leading socialists from the masses, while Mills and his compatriots hold that the power elite infiltrate parties of the Left *and* Right.

Finally, I argue that scholars of democratic party politics tend to assume an impermeable boundary around parties that separates them from the state and social movements. I point out, however, that classical party-centered theorists, including Weber and Michels, are the exceptions to this tendency. In the Iron Rule tradition, parties vie for control of the state, and the state meanwhile is strengthened as successive parties compete to wield its power. Thus, for the first time in this book, we encounter something approaching a theory of party-state relations. At the same time, the Iron Rule presupposes that parties are aloof even from allied social movements. In Michels' work, the German socialist party was once also a workers' movement, but the party-movement exists only for a minute, because the demands of organization result in the estrangement of the political leadership from the workers. Additionally, when the socialists became an official opposition party, Michels says, they simultaneously became "a state within a state," or a government-in-waiting. Thus, the socialists are a party-movement only briefly, after which they become entrenched in the state, but they are never a party-state-movement or omnibus party.

5

The Functional Party

In stark contrast to the last chapter, the works that appear below suggest first, that democracy is possible, and second, that parties are good for democracy. Parties are thus "functional," as opposed to dysfunctional, with respect to a free society. Scholars have made this argument in at least four prominent ways.

The first, which is the namesake of this chapter, is the functional parties tradition proper. Its central claim is that states and constitutions by themselves are unable to accomplish democracy; parties, because they must maintain organizational discipline to mobilize voters and thereby take or retain state power, make democratic governments do what they are supposed to do: serve the people (Rossiter 1960; Schattschneider [1942] 1967; Wilson 1905). The second is the responsible parties tradition, which suggests that when parties do their duty, they offer the mass electorate a meaningful choice of two or more policy alternatives on issues of national importance (American Political Science Association 1950; Key [1961] 1964; Schattschneider [1960] 1983). The next literature is what I call "elite but functional parties," and is sometimes called "the elitist theory of democracy" or "democratic elitism." The central analytical move here is to concede that parties are as oligarchical as Michels says they are (see pp. 85–7), but to insist in the next breath that *competition* among internally oligarchical organizations makes societies more democratic (Duverger [1951] 1963; Schumpeter [1942] 1975). The fourth theoretical tradition is pluralism. Though often lumped together with elite theories of democracy for good reasons, I maintain that the emphasis of pluralism is ever so slightly at variance with Schumpeter, for example, who is sometimes seen as the founder of the pluralist tradition. With respect to the relationship between parties and democracy, pluralists have a two-step argument. Their primary claim is that to the extent that elites exist, they are divided in myriad ways and are, in any case, accountable to interest groups, whose support they require, creating a sea of conflicting interests, in which no one group can dominate. Political parties, then, are proof of this primary claim, because while they tend to be dominated by a small leadership elite, the elites themselves first, come from the largest working-class ethnic communities, and second, have no choice but to support policies that such communities demand of their elected representatives (Dahl 1961; Polsby 1963). Finally, although there are four traditions, I have included here a fifth section devoted to possibly the most important contemporary sociologist of political parties, the late Seymour Martin Lipset. I do this for several reasons, but mainly because he straddles all the other traditions in this chapter. This is because his own politics and thinking changed during the mid-twentieth century, when the functional approach held sway. For example, in 1956, when he published *Union Democracy*, he sounded very much like a pluralist, but by 1962, when he published his introduction to a new edition of Michels' *Political Parties*, he had clearly become a democratic elitist. Throughout this period, however, he maintained the overall view that competitive party systems comprised the essential condition enabling the stability and survival of democratic society.

Functional Parties

Perhaps the earliest example of the functional parties tradition is Woodrow Wilson's (1905) *Constitutional Government in the United States*. Wilson defines constitutional government as "one whose powers have been adapted to the interests of its people and to the maintenance of individual liberty" (1905: 2). That form of government, he writes, arose in the thirteenth century with the Magna Carta, a pact signed by British nobles and King John outlining the terms under which the former would submit to the latter's rule. Because the king could no longer do as he pleased, Wilson says that the Magna Carta's effect was to make "government an instrument of the general welfare rather than an arbitrary, self-willed master" (1905: 3). Thus was born the "Whig theory" of constitutional government, according to which the rule of the executive must be checked by some institutional counterweight.

Whig theory greatly shaped the doctrine of "separation of powers" in the U.S. Constitution, which famously established checks and balances on supreme authority. It is a doctrine designed to create perfect equipoise, with no one branch of government dominating another. But in a move that is typical of the functional parties tradition, Wilson points out that the constitution is inadequately designed for democratic government. It does not (a) staff the thousands of offices of the federal government; (b) encourage cooperation among the countervailing branches; or (c) generate national judgments on national questions. Only the political party, which is outside the government and constitution, can perform these vital tasks (1905: 210). The hierarchy, nominations, and patronage that are endemic to the party machinery supply the elected representatives and political appointees who staff the government. As for the separation of powers, Wilson insists that the executive and legislative branches "cannot remain checked and balanced against one another; they must act, and act together." This is made possible by the mechanism of party discipline, which, through an elaborate system of rewards and punishments, socializes people within and across branches to collaborate with one another (1905: 211). Finally, because Congressmen and senators represent the interests of their states and districts, the legislature by itself is ill equipped to respond to national problems. Accordingly, Wilson observes, without parties "it would have hardly been possible for the voters of the country to be united in truly national judgments upon national questions" (1905: 217).

Like Wilson's work, E. E. Schattschneider's *Party Government* points to the gaps in democratic theory, though his is a dual emphasis on the antipartyism of early theorists like James Madison and the assumption that society would automatically express its will without the aid of political organization. Madison held that "parties were intrinsically bad, and the sole issue for discussion was the means by which bad parties might be prevented from becoming dangerous" ([1942] 1967: 8). The preventative measures as set forth in the U.S. Constitution were not only the separation of powers, but also the creation of a "large republic," whereby "as a consequence of the multiplicity of interests, no one of them is likely to win a majority" ([1942] 1967: 9). Madison's assumption was that smothering parties with a multitude of irreconcilable local interests would create the conditions under which society's will could express itself in its purest form. "Everyone took it for granted," writes Schattschneider, "that the people themselves would assume responsibility for the expression of their own will as a matter of course" ([1942] 1967: 14).

But Schattschneider insists that this assumption "involves a colossal oversimplification of the democratic process," in that it failed to anticipate "the difficulties arising from the numbers, preoccupation, immobility, and indifference of the people." As such, the classical definition of democracy "left a great, unexplored, undiscovered breach in the theory of modern government, the zone between the sovereign people and the government which is the habitat of the parties" ([1942] 1967: 14).

What function, then, do parties perform in the zone between the people and their government? Schattschneider argues that in the course of "party competition," they "organize the electorate and channelize the expression of the popular will" where otherwise the popular will would find no expression at all in the cacophony of the many and varied local interests. In this, Schattschneider advances an unqualified "defense of parties," because for him party government has worked to democratize the United States over the objections and constraints imposed by the constitution. Hence, the most famous and oft-cited passage in *Party Government*: "It should be stated flatly at the outset that this volume is devoted to the thesis that the political parties created democracy and that modern democracy is unthinkable save in terms of the parties" ([1942] 1967: 1, 3, 4).

Clinton Rossiter's (1960) thesis in *Parties and Politics in America* is similar to Schattschneider's in that parties are said to be existentially bound to the fate of American democracy. Hence, Rossiter's famous dictum: "NO America without democracy, no democracy without politics, no politics without parties, no parties without compromise and moderation" (1960: 1; emphasis in original). This claim suggests that parties perform several key functions that enable democracy to persist, chief among these being, "to control and direct the struggle for power." Parties perform this function by institutionalizing the struggle with organization, publicizing it by means of platforms and appeals, and, most important of all, stabilizing it through regular elections (1960: 39).

But if this is the political party's primary function, there are also a series of "subsidiary functions" that the party undertakes to connect the people to their government. Similar to Wilson, Rossiter observes that constitutions provide little help in staffing the many positions that enable the government to serve society. The political party steps into the breach by acting as an "immense personnel agency" (1960: 40). Contrary to the oligarchical party approach, which suggests that the doling out of government jobs inculcates political dependency and thereby perpetuates the domination of society by politicians (see pp. 76, 86, 93–7), Rossiter says that patronage serves an additional purpose "in acting as important buffers and adjusters between individuals and society." Parties are "important dispensers of those aids, favors, and immunities . . . that make it possible for men and women to live reasonably confident lives in a harsh environment" (1960: 48–9). Lastly, parties also translate the wants and needs of society into practical legislation. They are in fact the "best fitted of all agencies to convert formless hopes or frustrations into proposals that can be understood . . . [and] approved by the people" (1960: 42).

Responsible Parties

Rossiter's work offers a useful entry point to a second literature, in the sense that parties are said to put proposals in front of the people for their approval. This aspect of democratic party politics is the focus of the responsible parties tradition. Its most famous and enduring touchstone is a report from the Committee on Political Parties of the American Political Science Association (APSA), entitled, "Toward a More Responsible Two-Party System" (1950). The committee, which was chaired by E.E. Schattschneider, outlined two problems with the political climate of the day. First, the tasks of government in both foreign policy (e.g., prosecuting the Cold War with the Soviet Union) and domestic policy (e.g., in administering the New Deal welfare state) had grown immeasurably in complexity and number. Yet second, in this time of grave consequence, the public has no conception as to which direction the country should go. The major parties in the United States were unable to meet these problems head on, the committee wrote, because each was a loose federation of largely autonomous local and state machines, and because, as a consequence of this internal incoherence, the two parties were virtually indistinguishable from one another.

Thus, the crucial pivot of the APSA report was the distinction between what the parties should be doing (performing their role) and what they are actually doing (ignoring their role and therefore being irresponsible). "The role of the political parties" is to "provide the electorate with a proper range of choice between alternatives of action," preferably through "effective formulation of general policies and programs." From there, society might then assist in choosing a direction for the country by elevating one of the two major parties to power. Given that the parties have fallen short in these respects, the APSA committee recommended: (1) a stronger two-party system, (2) better integrated parties, and (3) more responsible parties. A stronger party system is one in which the parties "are able to bring forth programs to which they commit themselves"; "possess sufficient internal cohesion to carry out these programs"; and provide for "effective opposition" (1950: 1). Better integrated parties are ones with "greater resistance to pressure" from outside interest groups and "strong and active campaign organizations," capable of sustaining "sufficient party loyalty" (1950: 2). Lastly, responsible parties are ones that are accountable not only to the general public, but also to their members (1950: 2). Together these reforms would bring the loose federations of sub-national parties into sync, coordinate the execution of the complex and multifarious tasks of modern government, and provide a substantive clash between the parties through which the general public might discern alternative courses of action.

The APSA report was therefore a programmatic call to action, designed to alarm academics, politicians, and voters alike. This is no more obvious than in a section of the report, titled "The Dangers of Inaction," in which the committee predicts that the status quo will eventuate in the disintegration of the two parties and the rise of extreme right- and left-wing organizations (1950: 13–14). Since parties are charged with the task of holding civil society together, they are not exactly the latter's reflection as voter-centered theories tend to imply, but autonomous agencies that, when at their best, can offer the public a clear choice on important issues. Nor is the American two-party system an incorrigible oligarchy, for the committee's recommendations presuppose that the major parties may yet redeem themselves.

Schattschneider's change in tone from *Party Government* (1942) to *The Semisovereign People* (1960), in my view reflects a shift from a functional to a responsible parties perspective. That is, whereas in 1942, Schattschneider held that parties were functioning as they should, by 1960, he seemed to suggest that parties were not. The turning point undoubtedly occurred much earlier, for he chaired the APSA committee that produced the report on responsible parties in 1950.

In the later work, he argued that the function of political parties in a democracy was to provide the mass electorate with a choice on which to weigh in. However, there is no guarantee that parties will give the public a *clear* choice, and to the extent that they do, there is a good chance that the choice will be a *trivial* one. Accordingly, he insists that a vibrant democracy is one in which parties are responsible, meaning that they provide the people an opportunity to participate in making *important* choices. Thus, Schattschneider defines democracy as

a competitive political system in which competing leaders and organizations define the alternatives of public policy in such a way that the
public can participate in the decision-making process." ([1960] 1983:
141; emphasis in original)

Two paragraphs later, he adds that the "exploitation" of conflict
"by *responsible* political leaders and organizations is the essence
of democracy" ([1960] 1983: 142; emphasis added). Democracy
therefore consists not only in partisan conflict, but conflict over
issues that truly matter.

His famous claim that *"organization is the mobilization of bias"*
must be understood in terms of this overall vision of democracy
(Schattschneider [1960] 1983: 71; emphasis in original). Taken
out of context, one might interpret this to mean that parties merely
divide people in their struggle for power – an assumption that is
more at home in the exclusive party approach as we shall see (see
p. 124). But, in fact, Schattschneider wants to say that parties
must be counted on to manage political conflict for the sake of
democracy. Accordingly, in the paragraph preceding the "mobilization of bias" thesis, he writes, "The crucial problem in politics
is the management of conflict. No regime could endure which
did not cope with this problem. All politics, all leadership and all
organization involves the management of conflict" ([1960] 1983:
71). The role of parties in a properly functioning democracy, then,
is not merely to divide, but to prevent conflict from escalating to
unmanageable levels.

V.O. Key's (1961) book, *Public Opinion and American
Democracy*, is sometimes viewed as an adjunct to the "elite but
functional" tradition below (see, for example, Bachrach 1967:
47–8; Walker 1966: 285n2), but in my view it belongs resolutely
in the responsible parties tradition. The book is also taken as
a contradiction to his later work in the *Responsible Electorate*
(1966) (see, for example, Margolis 1977: 33), which I reviewed
in chapter 3 (see pp. 61–2), but I see the 1961 and 1966 works
as complementary.[1] In both cases, the mass electorate is not to be
blamed for what he viewed at the time as a state of confusion in
American politics. Not unlike the APSA report, Key insists that it

is irresponsible parties that are to blame. The oft-quoted central claim of the book is the following:

> the critical element for the health of a democratic order consists in the beliefs, standards, and competence of those who constitute the influentials, the opinion-leaders, the political activists in the order. (Key [1961] 1964: 558)

Very much as he suggests in the *Responsible Electorate*, then, Key asserts that the voice of the people is "an echo" of the political elite. That elite, however, "refuses to define itself with great clarity in the American system." Accordingly, if the democracy as a whole "tends toward indecision, decay, and disaster," he maintains, then "the responsibility rests here, not in the mass of the people" ([1961] 1964: 558).

Elite but Functional Parties

The foundational work in this third tradition is Joseph Schumpeter's (1942) *Capitalism, Socialism and Democracy*. A critique of classical democratic theory, the point of the book is to problematize the notion that "'the people' hold a definite and rational opinion about every individual question and that they give effect to this opinion – in a democracy – by choosing 'representatives' who will see to it that that opinion is carried out." The initiative and decisiveness of the mass electorate in a democracy has no basis in empirical reality, however, says Schumpeter. More accurately, the electorate chooses among groups of political elites who are in competitive struggle with one another, and those elites then more or less autonomously form and direct the government. Modern democracy is, in other words, a two-step process in which the people influence their government only indirectly. Thus, he writes, "the role of the people is to produce a government, or else an intermediate body which in turn will produce a national executive." This alternative view of democracy is truer, if less romantic, because it provides "for a proper recognition of the vital fact of leadership," which classical democratic theory essentially ignored ([1942] 1975: 269–70).

Now because Schumpeter seeks to bring political leaders into the equation, parties are central to his alternative theory of democracy, for contrary to classical theory, "the true function of the electorate's vote," he says, is the "acceptance of leadership" ([1942] 1975: 273). Schumpeter's problem with the electorate is that it has a limited repertoire of expression, "incapable of action other than a stampede" ([1942] 1975: 283). Parties therefore perform an invaluable function in the course of "competitive struggle for the people's vote," namely, to "regulate political competition" by offering up leaders to whom the people choose to submit.

In this, Schumpeter's vision is neither voter-centered, nor strictly oligarchical. Society itself is not the motive force behind politics. It is, rather, leadership, and specifically as provided by political parties. This is the reason that scholars sometimes refer to Schumpeter's framework as the "elitist" theory of democracy or democratic "elitism." Schumpeter goes as far as to say, "The psycho-technics of party management and party advertising, slogans and marching tunes, are not accessories. They are the essence of politics. So is the political boss" ([1942] 1975: 282–3). Schumpeter therefore shares something in common with Michels in the double sense that parties act at some considerable remove from their constituents, and constituents for their part are only minimally involved in the democratic process. Contrary to Michels, however, party oligarchy is not damaging to democracy for Schumpeter, but central to its functioning as it actually exists.

Schumpeter's view of parties finds a strong echo in Maurice Duverger's canonical work, *Political Parties*. The latter is best known for "Duverger's Law," according to which "*the simple-majority single-ballot system favours the two-party system*," but in fact the book is about much more than electoral rules ([1951] 1963: 217; emphasis in original). Taken as a whole, "It is essentially the study of party institutions and their place in the State" ([1951] 1963: xv).

Much of the book in fact reads like Michels. The "internal

structure" of political parties, he writes, "is essentially autocratic and oligarchic" ([1951] 1963: 422). But *Political Parties* is not a rehashing of the Iron Rule either. Oligarchy is only half the argument: Duverger writes about party organization in order to explain the function of party in relation to the state and civil society, and that function is actually *democratizing* in tendency. What, then, is the function of parties?

> The deepest significance of political parties is that they tend to the creation of new elites, and this restores to the notion of representation its true meaning, the only real one. All government is by nature oligarchic but the origins and the training of the oligarchs may be different and these determine their actions. The formula "Government of the people by the people" must be replaced by this formula "Government of the people *by an elite sprung from the people*". A regime without parties ensures the permanence of ruling elites chosen by birth, wealth, or position ... A regime without parties is of necessity a conservative regime ... it is further removed from democracy than the party regime. ([1951] 1963: 425–6; emphasis in original)

In this passage, Duverger contends that parties ensure government of the people by leaders drawn from the people. Without parties, governments are inherently conservative, because they are run by ruling elites, whose authority in government is derived from "birth, wealth, or position." This claim stands in opposition to Michels, for whom the circulation of a few leaders through positions of power is a sham democracy (see pp. 86–7). Michelsian observers of American politics might point out, for instance, that every presidential candidate between 1988 and 2012 graduated from either Harvard or Yale and that the leading contenders in that time were drawn principally from two families, the Clintons and the Bushes. For Duverger, however, the circulation of elites is the primary way by which parties, especially working-class parties, keep state power out of the hands of the aristocracy or at least force the latter to share state power. Thus, against the preceding claim about elite universities and political families, Duverger loyalists might point out that Bill Clinton and Barack Obama grew up in working-class households; that without the mechanism of the Democratic Party neither could have hoped to occupy the Oval Office; and that their class background predisposes them to govern on behalf of workers, whereas the Bushes, by virtue of their affluence, rule on behalf of the rich. The tension between party and society is palpable in Duverger, for parties operate at some remove from society, yet also ensure, by their control of the nominations process and other means, that the less affluent sectors of society are represented in the state.

Pluralism

The patriarch of the pluralist tradition in the United States is, without question, Robert Dahl, author of the famous case study of New Haven politics, *Who Governs?*. Pluralist democracy, which is the political system that Dahl claims prevails in New Haven, is one in which no one group of people dominates; instead political life is characterized by the interdependence of political, social, and economic elites, the sub-leaders and interest groups among them, and by extension the public as a whole. His target in that work is C. Wright Mills' *The Power Elite* (see pp. 87–8). If Mills held that a cohesive elite of corporate and military leaders had infiltrated the party system, Dahl showed in contrast that while elites undoubtedly exist, there are different sets of elites, who do not form a cohesive whole and are actually not especially interested in party politics.[2] The three sets of elites are the "political stratum," who are the staff members and elected representatives affiliated with the major parties; "social notables," who are the old Yankee families of New Haven, membership among whom is indicated by inclusion in the New Haven Lawn Club; and "economic notables," membership among whom is indicated by a certain level of property ownership as well as inclusion on corporate boards, the Chamber of Commerce, and the like. Dahl's point is that inequality exists but that the resources of elite status are not "cumulative;" that is, the resources of social nobility do not translate into economic nobility and, in turn, do not translate into dominance in the political world. Thus, "Out of nearly 500 elective and party offices in New Haven, in 1957–1958," he finds that social notables "held only two – both minor positions in the Republican party." Moreover, he points out that "about 5 percent of the total number" were both social and economic notables at the same time. Finally, his data suggest that among economic notables, only six were involved in political parties (1961: 64, 68, 69).

To the extent that parties have been infiltrated at all, they have been infiltrated by those he calls "ex-plebes," former working-class Jews, Italians, and Irish. Indeed, he finds that "the three largest ethnic groups" were "over-represented in elective posts." For Dahl, this indicates that the political stratum is easily "penetrated" and therefore tends to reflect the electorate. "In an open pluralistic system," he writes, "where movement into the political stratum is easy, the stratum embodies many of the most widely shared values and goals in society." Further, democracy obtains despite the control of the party apparatus by a small unaccountable leadership, because winning elections requires the enactment of policies that "reflect the preference of the populace . . . even if the policies of political associations were usually controlled by a tiny minority of leaders." Accordingly, he writes, though political leadership has passed from a "patrician oligarchy" of Mayflower elites to ethnic machine elites, New Haven has nevertheless become "a pluralist system" (1961: 44, 86, 91–2, 101).

Dahl's study is the most famous of three companion studies on New Haven. A second, slightly less famous piece is by Dahl's student, Nelson Polsby – *Community Power and Political Theory* (1963). The book is more a methodological critique of community studies in sociology than an empirical work like Dahl's. In it, Polsby makes a case for studying power through the lens of "behaviorism," according to which the analyst must observe people *doing* something before making any claims about power or other social dynamics. Thus, according to Polsby, to prove that "the power elite" exists, one must (a) examine public issues; (b) demonstrate that those issues are in fact important to the community in question; and (c) show that in an overt conflict between the preferences of an elite few and those of the non-elite many, decisions are made in the elite's favor every time or with sufficient regularity that one might plausibly claim the existence of a power differential (1963: 120–1).

However, when one applies these behaviorist criteria as Polsby does, it becomes clear that in New Haven and other American cities, no "power elite" has been proven to exist. If political power reflects any social identity, then it more reliably reflects ethnic belonging. Polsby writes, "New Haven's population is still clustered residentially more or less according to ethnic groups, and the ward political organizations and nominees for alderman reflect these clusters" (1963: 81). It bears mention here that Polsby does not object to the notion that politics in general reflects the make up of society; rather he objects to the twin notion associated with Mills that America is fundamentally a *class* society and that therefore Americans are dominated by a ruling class.

But to suggest that political parties reflect the relative strength of ethnic groups would be incomplete for Polsby, because ethnicity is merely one of a constellation of divisions that make up American society. For Polsby, as for pluralist scholars in general, "*nobody* dominates in a town" (1963: 113, 116; emphasis in original). This is because "Pluralists . . . see American society as fractured into a congeries of hundreds of small special interest groups, with incompletely overlapping memberships, widely differing power bases, and a multitude of techniques for exercising influence on decisions salient to them" (1963: 118). In this landscape of thoroughly "fragmented government," where one group may defeat a second group but then be defeated by a third, political parties above all reflect the ever changing and competing interests of multiple and evolving groups of Americans, such that even "the claims of small, intense minorities are usually attended to" (1963: 118).

The Special Case of Seymour Martin Lipset

The notion of a stable democracy anchored in multifarious conflicts and bases of power is consistent with Seymour Martin Lipset's vision of democratic party politics. I write in chapter 1 of this book that scholars incorrectly view Lipset as a mere extension of the Columbia model of electoral behavior (see pp. 22–3). In this, my treatment of him is at variance with much received wisdom on Lipset's work, and it is partly for this reason he receives (and I think rightly so, whatever my heretical comments) the longest section devoted to any one author in this book. By this I do not mean to suggest that Lipset somehow rejected the department that trained him. On the contrary, in a retrospective essay on his travels after graduate school, he would write, "Wherever I went thereafter, I would always be a product of Columbia sociology" (Lipset 1996: 13). Though he was an early co-author of Lazarsfeld (Lipset et al. 1954) and borrowed from the latter methodologically (e.g., the panel study and deviant case analysis), we must understand that Lipset was gesturing toward his adviser, Robert K. Merton, to whom he dedicated the aforementioned essay (Lipset 1996: 1). Of him, Lipset wrote, "Merton was to become the most important intellectual influence on me in my academic career" (1996: 7). This is an important data point, because Merton was a pillar of the functionalist tradition in sociology, according to which parties comprised a political sub-system or organ that regulated social conflict and thereby sustained the larger "social system."

That he was a functionalist, however, is not controversial; what is controversial is the claim that he distanced himself from the sociological approach to political behavior. To repeat, the sociological approach held that vote choice turned on loyalty to social group or "social cleavages." That is, to explain why some people vote one way and other people vote another way, the analyst need only ask them about their social relationships and their class, ethnic, and residential background (see p. 19). Let me begin, therefore, with the smoking gun. In 1959, Lipset criticized the Columbia voting studies, because

"the focus on cleavage . . . tends to direct voting research away from sociological concerns toward social psychology, since the actual research is designed to find out how various structural cleavages affect the decision of the individual . . . emphasis on the integrative aspects of electoral behavior would not only fill lacunae in our understanding of democracy as a system but would necessarily be more sociological in orientation than the study of cleavage." (Buxton 1985: 228; Lipset [1959] 1965: 92–3)

The emphasis on social cleavages, therefore, privileged the individual as the primary unit of analysis. That is, the point of the Columbia voting studies was to predict with some reliability how any one person would likely cast their ballot on the basis of their social background and relationships. Though he held generally to the claim that cleavages shaped individual political allegiances, Lipset nevertheless categorized this preoccupation as fundamentally social psychological, not sociological. A truly *sociological* theory would de-emphasize the determinants of vote choice, in favor of examining how "democracy as a system" is integrated. Lipset's work from *Union Democracy* (1956)[3] through *Party Systems and Voter Alignments* (1967) argues consistently that the institution most important in performing the function of integration in the democratic system is a competitive party system.

Lipset, Trow, and Coleman's (1956) *Union Democracy* is about an organization that deviates from the iron rule, the International Typographical Union (ITU). Contrary to Michels' prediction that "private governments" (e.g., parties, unions) would descend into oligarchy because of the demands of organization (see p. 87), the authors found that the ITU maintained a robust democratic union. The book thus explains how the union was able to defy the iron rule. As he would in his later works, Lipset and his associates "aimed at identifying the factors which make for and sustain democracy" (Lipset et al. 1956: 413).

By far the essential and decisive factor in preserving democracy in the ITU, they argued, was an institutionalized two-party system. That is, instead of voting on a single leadership slate (a common practice in unions and parties), ITU members vote for one of two parties. Thus, parties are functional or enabling of democracy provided that they express and channel competing cleavages or sets of cleavages and provided, therefore, that no one group – especially the leadership stratum – is able to dominate the entire organization or society. They write, "Perhaps the most important democratic defense mechanism which has been institutionalized in the ITU is the two-party system itself. The sheer existence of a two-party system provides one of the principal opportunities and stimulations for participation in politics by the members of an organization or community" (1956: 401). In "one-party unions" by contrast, "apathy on the part of the members is functional to the stability of the incumbent machine" (1956: 402).

Lipset's book *Political Man* (1960) is by far his most influential and is taken to represent a reassertion of the sociological approach to political behavior. As evidence of this, analysts often cite the admittedly infelicitous claim that "parties . . . basically represent a 'democratic translation of the class struggle'" (Lipset 1960: 230). I would maintain, however, that this is a functionalist argument taken out of context, for *Political Man* is really a book about the conditions that enable "conflict within consensus," especially the ability of political parties to integrate otherwise irresolvable antagonisms into a stable democracy. He writes,

> One of political sociology's prime concerns is an analysis of the social conditions making for democracy. Surprising as it may sound, a stable democracy requires the manifestation of conflict or cleavage so that there will be struggle over ruling positions, challenges to parties in power, and shifts of parties in office; but without consensus – a political system allowing the peaceful "play" of power, the adherence of the "outs" to decisions made by the "ins," and the recognition by the "ins" of the rights of the "outs" – there can be no democracy. The study of the conditions encouraging democracy must therefore focus on the sources of both cleavage and consensus. (1960: 1)

The central question then is: "How can a society face continuous conflict among its members and groups and still maintain social cohesion and the legitimacy of state authority?" His answer, as the foregoing infamous quote suggests, is that parties channel the class struggle into elections. Quoting Talcott Parsons, the leading functionalist of Merton's generation, Lipset states that, "the study of politics cannot be 'treated in terms of a specifically specialized conceptual scheme . . . precisely for the reason that the political problem of the social system is a focus for the integration of all of its analytically distinguished components.'" The "underlying dilemma," therefore, is "the proper balance between conflict and consensus," and, he adds, "It is the central problem with which this book deals" (Lipset 1960: 3–4; Parsons 1951: 126–7). Neither *Political Man* nor any other of Lipset's early works, then, is voter-centered in the way that *The People's Choice* (Lazarsfeld et al. [1944] 1948) and *Voting* (Berelson et al. 1954) were (see pp. 19–22). Instead, Lipset's primary focus was the process by which political parties balanced conflict and consensus in democratic systems.

If in these earlier works, Lipset articulated a pluralist model of this vision, then by 1962, six years after the publication of *Union Democracy*, it was clear that Lipset had taken a page out of Schumpeter and Duverger. In that year, Lipset published his introduction to a new edition of Michels' *Political Parties*, in which he advanced what he explicitly called, "the 'elitist' theory of democracy" to stand as an alternative to Michels' iron rule (Lipset 1962: 33). Significantly, Lipset dropped his wish for democratic organizations like the ITU, arguing instead that *even if* parties are oligarchical, the contribution of *competing* oligarchical organizations representing divergent interests is to protect and maintain democracy. Accordingly, he halfway concedes,

> While most . . . political parties will remain one-party systems . . . it is important to recognize that many internally oligarchic organizations help to sustain political democracy in the larger society and to protect the interests of their members from the encroachment of other groups. Democracy in large measure rests on the fact that no one group is able to secure a basis of power and command over the majority so that it can effectively suppress or deny the claims of the groups it opposes. (Lipset 1962: 36–7)

For example, oligarchical parties like Michels' own German socialist party have been responsible for countless improvements in the lives of the mass electorate such as the freedom of speech, freedom of movement, and guarantees of job security, to say nothing of the equalization of income and opportunity. This is meant to suggest that both Michels and C. Wright Mills are prematurely pessimistic of the possibility of democracy (Lipset 1962: 35–6). Indeed, for

Lipset, since the publication of Mills' *The Power Elite* (see pp. 87–8), sociology as a whole had become far too preoccupied with conflict, cleavage, change, and social disintegration. Lipset's introduction to *Political Parties*, like his other work from this period, was intended to check this trend by concentrating more on the conditions of social integration (Buxton 1985: 230).

Lipset's more mature work in this direction, however, and undoubtedly the last truly original programmatic statement in the sociology of democratic party politics, was his introduction (with Stein Rokkan) to an edited volume called, *Party Systems and Voter Alignments* (1967). In a work of grand comparative and historical sweep, Lipset and Rokkan delineated the functions of political parties in a democratic order and theorized the social origins of party systems in Western Europe. Parties, they wrote, serve an *"expressive* function" in that "they develop a rhetoric for the translation of contrasts in the social and the cultural structure into demands and pressures for action or inaction." They also possess *"instrumental* and *representative* functions" in that parties force the leaders of competing interest groups to bargain with each other, stagger their demands over time, and occasionally join forces to exert the maximum pressure on the state (1967: 5; emphasis in original). In all these ways, parties work to enable the smooth operation of democracy in the face of potentially divisive "contrasts."[4]

Lipset and Rokkan then pair the overarching functionalist framework with a historical narrative that traces the origins of competing interest groups to two types of "critical juncture" in Western Europe: national revolution and industrial revolution. Using Parsons' analytic strategy of comparing cases across polarities (Lipset 1996: 16–17), Lipset and Rokkan identified four types of partisan cleavage: majority vs. minority ethnic groups; nation-state vs. church; landowning vs. industrial elites; and eventually the overriding one, elites vs. non-elites (1967: 14–15). It bears mention that, for them, parties do not spring spontaneously from revolutionary movements: whether and how they do so depends on several institutional variables such as "incorporation" (i.e., whether or not the supporters of the social movement have citizenship rights on a par with their opponents after the revolution). The implication is that if the level of incorporation is high, social movement demands will be channeled more seamlessly into the party system. Finally, forever linked to this account of European cleavage formation is Lipset and Rokkan's "freezing hypothesis," according to which revolutionary era cleavages became entrenched in the 1920s and comprised the grist of competitive party politics in Western Europe thereafter (1967: 50).

*

If, as I have argued, one must understand sociology's contribution to understand the field as a whole, then this chapter is especially illustrative. One cannot understand the economist and political scientist, Joseph Schumpeter, for example, unless one understands his commonalities and differences with Michels and Duverger, who were both sociologists. Likewise, one cannot fully appreciate the pluralists without knowing that their interlocutors were sociologists in the power elite tradition. And certainly, one would be insufficiently oriented, if one were not familiar with the contributions of Seymour Martin Lipset, a sociologist so influential in the field of party politics that he served as president of the American Political Science Association. Further, to reiterate my second point, none of the debates or intellectual movements in this chapter can be reduced to the Columbia voter studies. They are resolutely party-centered, where the Columbia model is voter-centered. In the former, the level of analysis is the institution; in the latter, it is the individual. The debate in this chapter turns on whether parties are a boon or a bane to democracy; in the Columbia studies, the debate is over which variable is the decisive determinant of vote choice. My third claim has been that a battle over disciplinary turf will impair our sense of where we have been and where we can go next. To say that one discipline has the right sensibility for studying party politics, while another has the wrong kind, would obscure the plain fact that in this chapter political scientists and sociologists have roughly the same vision of the relationship between party and society. At the same time, the mortal antagonism between the functional and oligarchical approaches provides further evidence for my fourth claim, which is that party-centered scholars are in conversation with each other, and not with the exponents of the dominant voter-centered approaches of the field. Lipset and possibly Key are the lone exceptions.

My fifth argument is that while the literature on democratic party politics tends to assume the radical separation of parties from the state and civil society, party-centered theorists supply the leading exceptions to this rule. Within the functional approach, the state and civil society show up in at least three distinct ways. In Schattschneider and Wilson, the state comprises the institutions that arose from the U.S. Constitution, and which are paradoxically inadequate to the task of democratic governance. Here, we get the sense that the state does some things, and parties do other things that make the state more responsive to society. The state and civil society show up in another way in Duverger. The state assumes a shape that is similar to that featured in the oligarchical approach, for it is something powerful that parties seek to wield. The state is also given to the rule of the few unless Left parties intervene to elevate the non-elite to power. This capacity to supplant affluent elites with a leadership sprung from the popular sectors of civil society is in fact the parties' central democratizing role, contrary to the claims of the iron rule tradition. Finally, in Lipset, the liberal democratic state is in the background as the thing that must be protected by political parties as they channel society's emergent tensions into the electoral process. As a result, however, parties are mediators between movements and the state and thus remain analytically separate. For Lipset, national or working-class revolutions are led by movements, whose interests are then expressed and mediated through parties, in a way that maintains the legitimacy of the state.

6

The Exclusive Party

By "exclusive," I do not mean to suggest that the traditions in this chapter view parties as "elite" in the sense of the oligarchical approach. Rather, if the distinguishing characteristic of political parties is that they are anti-democratic as they are in chapter 4, and essential for democracy as they are in chapter 5, then in this chapter, the distinguishing characteristic of parties is that they *differentiate* their own interests and identities from those of other parties. That is, a party's leaders, operatives, and rank-and-file do not see themselves as one with humankind – there may be a pretense that a party represents the great majority of "the people," but even in those cases, the party sets itself apart from its adversary, often by suggesting that the latter represents a tiny, nefarious minority.[1]

The way in which differentiation is accomplished diverges by tradition, however. The literature on legislative coalitions suggests that parties tend to form competing coalitions instead of one grand coalition, because they discover in the course of political practice that it is the rational thing for legislators to do. It is in their *interest* as utility-maximizing individuals to organize themselves against other groups, because doing so allows them to win more of what they want, whether that be the spoils of office or the realization of one's policy agenda (Aldrich 1995; Dodd 1976; Poole and Rosenthal 1997; Riker 1962; Valelly 2004). I conceive of a second set of works as an important interlude between the legislative and Marxist traditions. The scholars in this sub-section tend to be critical of the notion that interests are "given." Whereas students of legislative coalitions assume that interests are "exogenously" defined, meaning defined outside the context of partisan struggle (e.g., a legislator votes as s/he does, because s/he comes from an industrial or rural state), these scholars hold that individual and group interests are defined, and therefore often shift, in the course of such struggle (Gerteis 2003, 2007; Redding 2003; Sartori 1969; Slez and Martin 2007). On the other side of this interlude is the Marxist tradition, which sees the political party as the most important vehicle for articulating an analysis of capitalism as a social order of the "haves" and "have nots" and for achieving the emancipation of subaltern groups, especially the working class. That marginalized peoples will spontaneously see themselves as an oppressed mass in struggle with a privileged few cannot be taken for granted, however, for parties may articulate any number of cleavages (e.g., class, nationality, gender, religion, etc.) as matters of contention as they struggle for hegemony (de Leon et al. 2009; Gramsci [1921] 2000, [1926] 1992, 1971; Lenin [1902] 1973; Przeworski 1977; Przeworski and Sprague 1986).

Legislative Coalitions

The theoretical foundation of this first tradition is William Riker's (1962) *The Theory of Political Coalitions*. The book was a reaction to the "traditional methods" of political science, including "history writing, the description of institutions, and legal analysis," which, he said, amounted to "wisdom and neither science nor knowledge" and have brought the discipline to a "cul-de-sac." Riker's ambition was to build a unified theory upon which political scientists could conduct empirical study (1962: viii–ix).

His framework draws on "game theory," which is inspired by Von Neumann and Morgenstern's (1944) theory of "n-person games." N-person games, on Riker's account, turn on two conditions: (1) rationality and (2) zero-sum games. The first is simply that people in a game want to win and act accordingly. The second, zero-sumness (which is generally not a feature of n-person games but is a feature of Riker's minimum winning coalitions), is that in a two-person game, for example, one player's gain is exactly equal to the other player's loss. In other words, there is no such thing as mutual gain (1962: 12–13).

Riker adapted game theory to party politics in a way that he hoped would pre-empt the objection that not all human action was rational. Riker cleverly concedes this point, but insists that there are *some* games such as elections and the formation of governing electoral coalitions, in which people do behave rationally. Those games are ones in which the players have a "fiduciary" responsibility to win, akin to the "fiduciary trust" of corporate boards who are bound by law to maximize the returns to their shareholders' investments. Likewise, party actors are bound to do everything in their power to win elections. The zero-sum condition applies to political games, because electoral victory is an indivisible unit – either you win elections or you lose them (1962: 20–3, 25–6, 30–1).

The central principle of Riker's game theoretic framework is "the size principle," which is more commonly known in the literature as the "minimum winning coalition." The principle reads as follows:

> *In social situations similar to n-person, zero-sum games . . . participants create coalitions just as large as they believe will ensure winning and no larger.* (1962: 32–3; emphasis in original)

That is, the members of a party will "maximize only up to the point of subjective certainty of winning. After that point they seek to minimize, that is, to maintain themselves at the size (as subjectively estimated) of a minimum winning coalition" (1962: 33). In other words, parties do not want or work towards consensus despite frequent calls for "bipartisanship" among American politicians. Rather, they prefer division between a bare majority coalition on the one hand, and a bare minority coalition on the other.

This may be counterintuitive to some, because after all, why wouldn't a political party do its best to win a maximum number of votes in the electorate and thereby win the maximum number of seats in the legislature? The answer is that barely winning increases the spoils or perks of office that can be divided among the members of the winning party. Having more people in the winning coalition only decreases the spoils that each member can have. Consider for a moment an election to a seven-person committee in which the majority party gets an apple pie. The minimum winning coalition in a simple majority game is four. If the party wins four seats, then the pie will be divided into four big pieces, but if the party wins all seven seats, then each member will get a smaller piece. Thus, Riker writes, "for any coalition larger than minimum, its members can, by ejecting one or more of their members, increase the amount to be divided among them. Since the ejection is presumably costless, in such a game only minimum winning coalitions can be expected to occur" (1962: 42).

Riker then draws on examples from American political history, in which a party has achieved almost total dominance of the political system. He writes that in every such instance, "the leaders of the party have in some way decreased its size, which is exactly what one would expect according to the size principle." For example, when President Andrew Jackson, the first leader of the modern Democratic Party, swept nearly all national, state, and local elections, he "drove out all who would not follow him until he achieved a tightly organized and almost minimal winning coalition" (1962: 65).

Thus, the relationship of political parties to the state and civil society in Riker's account is clearly at odds with that proposed by the functional party approach in two ways. For Riker, a party's approach to government is fundamentally one of "office-seeking," where party members strive above all to achieve minimum winning coalitions so that each member reserves to herself the largest possible portion of the spoils. Correspondingly, parties are not motivated by the social function of connecting the people to their government, but rather by the prospect of using the people's votes to maximize the perks of office. Accordingly, office-seeking scholars have conducted cross-national studies to show that political parties aim for minimum winning coalitions, and that such coalitions, presumably because they play the game the best and are therefore more tightly organized, are stronger than those that aim for the maximum. For example, Lawrence Dodd (1976) argues that governments formed on the basis of the size principle tend to last longer.

In contrast to Riker, for whom legislative coalitions seek only the emoluments of office, Aldrich argued that politicians established the first political parties in the United States in order to overcome the challenges of organizing large numbers of rational actors, and thereby not only share in the spoils of office, but also achieve their policy agendas.[2] This happened in two phases.

Politicians first formed "legislative parties" to coordinate collective action among themselves in the legislature. Thus, "parties-in-government" surfaced when legislators discovered that they could achieve their individual goals more efficiently when they worked with like-minded colleagues. "A series of problems that necessarily arise in elections and in governance," he writes, "make it possible for politicians to win more of what they seek to win, more often, and over a longer period by creating political parties." As an example of this kind of budding organization, Aldrich calls the 1800 U.S. presidential election "a contest between two broad-scale and reasonably integrated teams of political elites contesting for power to achieve in part the goals of the party" (Aldrich 1995: 28; 2005: 26)

Party formation enters a second phase when legislators make another discovery: that they can strengthen their position in parliament by rallying public support for their policies. This, however, forces legislative parties to confront a different collective action problem: organizing the electorate. To do this, party elites must take the extra step of forming national networks of local organizations consisting of party cadres (e.g., precinct captains) and regular voters. Thus, Aldrich observes that the founders of the Democratic Party in the United States built the National Alliance and Caucus in the 1830s to link their legislative organizations with a "party-in-the-electorate" (Aldrich 1995: 47–50, 97, 100–25).

To be fair there is more to Aldrich's account of the transition from legislative to mass parties than rational action, in that he views the intrinsic value of voting (e.g., "citizen duty" or "being known to be on the right side") as part of the calculus of early American voters. Nevertheless, Aldrich frames matters of principle or loyalty as one among a complex of factors that "lessen the costs" of mass party affiliation. Most importantly, Aldrich's focus remains the self-interest of elites, who above all understood that "control of a majority in the public brought control of office, and with that, control of policy and the spoils of office" (1995: 100–2).

Like Riker, Poole and Rosenthal's (1997) book, *Congress*, focuses on the dynamics of winning coalitions, but for them the latter's hallmark is not that they are "minimum" or bare majorities as Riker held, but that they are "flexible." Drawing on Converse's concept of ideological constraint, they define a flexible coalition as one that votes together across a range of issues. When such coalitions are stable (i.e., if they vote together with some regularity over time), it is possible, they say, to describe legislators across a liberal to conservative continuum. For example, one might reliably say that until the end of the 112th Senate (Jan. 3, 2013), John Kerry (Democrat from Massachusetts) was a liberal Democrat, Max Baucus (Democrat from Montana) was a moderate Democrat, Olympia Snowe (Republican from Maine) was a moderate Republican, and Chuck Grassley (Republican from Iowa) was a conservative Republican. When the ideology of legislators is this well-known and their votes are correspondingly this predictable, it is also possible to explain the roll call votes of the entire U.S. Congress, using spatial theory's unidimensional scale of liberal to conservative or left to right. That is, roll call votes can be represented as splits on the liberal to conservative continuum, where everyone on one side of a critical point votes one way, and everyone to the other side votes the opposite way. When the critical point is to the left of the median voter (in this case, a legislator), then the conservative coalition wins. In the example above, Max Baucus and other like-minded Democrats vote with the Republicans. Conversely, when the critical point is to the right of the median voter, then the liberal coalition wins. Here it would be Olympia Snowe and like-minded Republicans joining the Democrats (Poole and Rosenthal 1997: 4–5).

Their key finding is that a unidimensional spatial model organized from liberal to conservative accounts for most of the winning coalitions in congressional history with the exceptions of the racial upheavals of the Civil War, Reconstruction, and civil rights when a second dimension, North vs. South, accounted for a substantial percentage of the variation (1997: 227). There are many implications for this finding, but for our purposes, the take-home message is that the U.S. Congress, with rare but significant exceptions, has split ideologically in nearly all the roll call votes in its history.

Their most famous finding, however, is that the ideological split in Congress has been widening in recent years. Congress is becoming more polarized (1997: 9, 80–5, 229–32). This is because each newly elected cohort of Republican legislators is becoming more conservative, while their Democratic counterparts from the South are becoming more liberal (1997: 9). After 1979, overlap between the median voters of each party (e.g., the Olympia Snowes) began to shrink: liberal Republicans and conservative Democrats became rarer (1997: 82). To put it more in terms of their model, beginning in the late-1970s, Congressional voting has become "increasingly unidimensional," that is, explainable in terms of ideology. For example, in the 102nd House (1991–1993), the liberal to conservative dimension "accounts for about 86 percent of the choices; in the 103rd House [1993–1995], 88 percent of the choices; and for the first session of the 104th House (1995), 90 percent of the choices." Meanwhile the importance of the second dimension (North vs. South), which peaked during the civil rights era, explains only an additional 1 percent of the voting. This, they say, is because voting on racial issues has been absorbed into the liberal to conservative continuum (1997: 230). Accordingly, they write, the U.S. Congress evinces "for the first time in nearly 60 years, two sharply distinct political parties," and add presciently, "Intense conflict between these two 'new' parties will continue" (1997: 232).

I end this sub-section with Richard Valelly's 2004 book, *The Two Reconstructions*, both because it offers an interesting spin on Riker's theory of winning coalitions, and because it is a nice segue into the next section. Valelly seeks to explain why the first reconstruction after the U.S. Civil War failed to permanently enfranchise blacks, whereas the second reconstruction, the Civil Rights Movement, succeeded (2004: ix, 7). He argues that there were three critical variables. The first, which is common to both reconstructions, is the formation of novel coalitions during party crisis. Valelly contends that the electoral game occasionally takes on a terrifying finality or "zero-sumness," where a party that does nothing to increase their base of support in the electorate will be in jeopardy. In response, parties do something daring: they enfranchise new voters to defeat the other side. Thus, following a revisionist application of Riker, Valelly argues, "coalition formation results if [political] elites believe that 'their long-term capacity to reproduce their elite status' is plainly and unmistakably jeopardized" (2004: 13). The second variable is "Black Political Will in Coalition-Making," which refers to the fact that African-Americans through their social movements were a crucial partner in coalition-making during both reconstructions (2004: 13).

But the decisive factor was a third variable: the relative ease of winning the vote using party-building and the courts. This was the only variable that differed across the two reconstructions. In the nineteenth century, the Republican Party engaged in "crash party-building" in their bid to enfranchise blacks in the South, where no Republican organization had previously existed. By contrast, in the twentieth century, the Democrats encountered a thorny but less difficult task: replacing white southern Democratic coalitions, which already controlled the South politically, with biracial ones. Additionally, as pro-civil rights forces took their fight to the courtroom, each coalition had to negotiate starkly different terrains. The nineteenth-century coalition was hit with a setback in the U.S. Supreme Court's first review of the black franchise, whereas the twentieth-century coalition was buoyed by initial judicial affirmation of the voting rights of blacks (2004: 17–18). Thus, in the 1950s and 1960s, coalition formation in party crisis, black mobilization, and institutional factors combined explosively to win and maintain the black franchise at last.

The Construction of Groups and Interests: A Theoretical Interlude

Valelly is a nice transition piece to consider as we move to a second literature. For Valelly, the overriding interest of party elites in moments of crisis is the maintenance of their status, which presumably anyone would prefer, regardless of the game being played. For example, it is plausible to assume that an employee, when faced with the prospect of demotion, might do something more entrepreneurial than usual to keep his position. The interest of maintaining status is, in other words, framed as a universalistic pursuit, akin to life and death, that anyone would engage in, though in this case it concerns the survival of one's political party. Yet interestingly, Valelly suggests that the rational motive driving coalition formation was not the decisive reason that the second reconstruction succeeded, where the first one failed. It was rather the historical unfolding of party building and jurisprudence that won the day in the twentieth century.

The scholars in this sub-section would take issue with Valelly's adherence to Riker, while applauding his historical argument. For them, interests are not pre-given by the supposedly primordial interest of wealth or utility maximization. To put it more technically, interests are not "exogenously" defined with respect to politics; interests are defined or constructed *within* politics, specifically by the struggle for power among political elites.

Let us take as an example Giovanni Sartori's famous essay, "From the Sociology of Politics to Political Sociology." Sartori's target is Lipset's claim in *Political Man* that parties reflect class antagonism (Sartori 1969: 71). He begins by questioning whether or not voters can be said to have a class identity when they themselves are unaware of that identity. If a worker does not see herself as a member of the working class, but say, as a woman, a Christian, or a Kenyan, then what right does the analyst have to "impute" or impose a class identity on her (Sartori 1969: 73–4)?

Sartori's alternative approach is to test what he calls an "organizational variable" that would map the "influence of party and trade union control" on voting behavior. In doing so, one might be able to confirm whether political parties organize workers to see themselves as a class or merely reflect what workers already realize based, say, on their experience of working in a factory. For instance, if an analyst finds that workers vote for the labor party in the absence of any local organizational influence (e.g., a labor party chapter), then we might say that parties have little to no influence on the inculcation of class identity and that therefore it is workers who exert upward pressure on parties to represent them (Sartori 1969: 84).

Once social scientists test this organizational variable, Sartori suspects that the data will contradict Lipset's findings (see p. 119). For him, a worker's position in the economic system only makes it easier or at least possible that workers will see themselves as a class. It is up to the parties to do the rest. Thus, Sartori wrote famously,

> To put it bluntly, it is not the "objective" class (class conditions) that creates the party, but the party that creates the "subjective" class (class consciousness). More carefully put, whenever parties reflect social classes, this signifies *more* about the party end than about the class end of the interaction. The party is not a "consequence" of the class. Rather, and before, it is the class that receives its identity from the party. Hence class behavior presupposes a party that not only feeds, incessantly, the "class image," but also a party that provides the structural cement of "class reality." (Sartori 1969: 84; emphasis in original)

Class therefore has no objective existence outside of party politics. Class is only ever an "image," "reality," and "identity" that is constructed by parties. It follows, then, that class is not the only way that society may be divided; a party may also use religion to divide people. Whether the people embrace one identity or another depends on which party wins the struggle to define society. He explains, "Whenever the class appeal outweighs the religious appeal, this is not because class is an 'objective reality'; rather, this is because the ideology of class wins the 'belief battle,' in conjunction with the prevalence of a new organizer, the mass party" (Sartori 1969: 87).

Sartori's work dovetails with the "political constructionist" literature. Like other social scientists, this school of thought assumes that race is "socially constructed." Race does not "exist" in any objective sense, but is rather created and maintained by people. As proof, scholars often point to the fluidity of racial categories over time, among and within groups, and across societies. If race were truly "real," one would expect to find some consistency along these axes of comparison, but instead we find diversity, inconsistency, and contradiction. For example, the Irish were once considered inferior to blacks in the American racial hierarchy but are considered "white" today. Racial categories in the United States, which turn on the binary between white and black, are not the same as those in Brazil, which refer to multiple gradations of skin tone and are freighted with different historical meanings.

But unlike other social scientists of race, political constructionists hold that racialization – the process by which people are assigned to an invented racial category – takes place in the political arena. The approach grew up partly in reaction to the assumption that the interests of different racial groups may be read off the so-called "objective conditions" in which they live. For example, under South African apartheid, where white Afrikaners supposedly benefited from enforced racial separation at the expense of "blacks" and "coloreds," such an analysis would expect whites to support apartheid and everyone else to oppose it. Political constructionists reject the idea that interests are necessarily given by objective conditions. A favorite case in point is the populist revolt of the late-nineteenth-century United States, in which white and black farmers joined forces to take over the political system. Rather than assume that these interracial farmer coalitions failed because whites and blacks had fundamentally conflicting interests, Gerteis demonstrates that black Republicans and white Democrats constructed "narratives of interest" that initially led farmers of different backgrounds to see each other as a collective. It was only after organizing problems surfaced that the two parties came to view the meaning of the coalition differently and dissolved it (Gerteis 2003: 199, 202).

Redding (2003) uses a similar approach to explain the disfranchisement of blacks and poor whites in North Carolina after the populist revolt. Dissatisfied with accounts that suggest that racial prejudice was its root cause, Redding argues that racism itself does not clarify how disfranchisement was actually accomplished. Thus, he writes, "Motive is not a mechanism," an explanation for what happened and why (2003: 6). As an alternative, Redding explains that the contraction of democratic rights at the turn of the twentieth century originated with the way in which political elites *made* race and power.

That process occurred in three phases. In the immediate post-Civil War period, Democratic Party elites in North Carolina forged a "vertical organization of power" that tied different sectors of the community together through a system of mutual obligations and benefits that kept wealthy whites on top and poor whites and blacks on the bottom. But in 1894 and 1896, a third-party fusion of Republicans and Populists defeated the Democratic Party with a "horizontal organization of power" by "stressing equality and denying the significance of hierarchy within the group." Finally, Democratic Party elites borrowed from their opponents' strategies by building horizontal camaraderie among whites through the rhetoric of "white supremacy" in 1898 and 1900. "Once back in power," Redding observes, "elite Democrats used the state to disfranchise, and therefore demobilize, their opponents" (Redding 2003: 14–16). In this, Redding joins Gerteis by questioning the explanatory power of objective racial interests. He writes,

> The absolute political relevance of certain categories of people (such as "class," "farmer," or even "race") – and the attendant interests that are lumped together with them – cannot be assumed. Instead, the analysis must trace how certain identities came to be thoroughly politicized . . . [and] came to be essential mechanisms of mobilization. (2003: 11)

Social identities and interests may therefore exist, but not until parties create them to divide people and thereby build power. To find the origins of political outcomes such as disfranchisement, then, one need look no further than the sphere of politics itself. "Political traditions and rules as well as party structures and activists," Redding argues, "are the primary organizers of political action" (2003: 11).

I end this section with an article by Slez and Martin (2007). Other explanations of the outcomes of the U.S. constitutional convention (which drafted the constitution in 1787) assume that the interests of individual delegates and states were defined "exogenously," that is, well before the delegates even met and the politicking began. For instance, on the question of representation, big states are assumed to prefer "representation by population," where each state would have a certain number of representatives in Congress based on the number of residents. Small states are accordingly assumed to favor "one state, one vote," so they would not be so easily outvoted by big states. Likewise, slave states were assumed to favor the slave trade, while free states were assumed to oppose it.

Slez and Martin argue instead for a *sequential* explanation, in which decisions or compromises on earlier questions fundamentally shift the meaning of later questions and, consequently, the very terrain of possible interests and alliances. Thus, they write, "Each step of the Convention, whereby some choices were solidified, changed the institutional context for further choices, and hence the constellation of interests, and hence the constellation of possible alliances" (2007: 63). Aptly they compare the process of collective choice to a "funnel," where the number of open questions at the beginning of the convention narrowed significantly by the middle and so on (2007: 62). For example, once the issue of the slave trade was decided, the strategic alliance between South Carolina and Georgia fractured over successive issues. Similarly, once the Connecticut Compromise was passed (i.e., "one state, one vote" in the Senate, but "rep by pop" in the House), elites would decide later votes based on that earlier agreement, rather than relitigating the issue of representation (2007: 62). Put another way, whereas previous analysts had attempted to explain these votes as each issue was put *on the table*, Slez and Martin stress the importance of issues that are *taken off table* in shifting interests and coalitions.

Most importantly for our purposes, this piece is crucial for understanding the formation of political parties after 1787, because the convention had settled (at least for two generations) questions that would otherwise have changed the constellation of interests and alliances for political struggle post-Convention. They write, "The elites, we might say, were successful not because they chose a structure that served 'their' interests, but because they set up an arena for the sorts of fights they wanted to have, and *could* have, within the framework of a nation" (2007: 63). Accordingly, in answer to the question, "Where do parties come from?" they answer, "Parties were, and, we argue, are, established in reference to a particular institutional structure that defines interests conditional on possible alliances and avenues of future political action" (2007: 65).

Marxism

Apropos of the construction of interests, the classical works of the Marxist tradition, especially those of Marx and Engels, may be read as taking class interests as given (i.e., as naturally proceeding from the structural antagonism between the bourgeoisie or capitalists and the proletariat or workers) and taking parties, therefore, as reflecting those interests. We concern ourselves with this "economic determinist" reading of Marx in the first half of the sub-section. In the second half, we turn to those Marxists who insist that interests and social divisions are constructed in the context of partisan struggle.

An "Economic Determinist" Reading of Karl Marx

There are many readings of Marx's work, but one influential interpretation is that it amounts to a theory of "economic determinism," the view that all non-economic phenomena such as religion, culture, and politics are really determined by economic factors such as a society's system of production. His thesis on party and society, written with Friedrich Engels, is laid out in the "Manifesto of the Communist Party." The key passages are found in the section, "Proletarians and Communists," where Marx and Engels specify the relationship between the party and the working class. The section is framed by the question, "In what relation do the Communists stand to the proletarians as a whole?" ([1848] 1998: 50). Their answer is two-fold.

First, Marx and Engels hold that there is a one-to-one correspondence between workers and the party. For example, they write, "The Communists . . . have no interests separate and apart from those of the proletariat as a whole. They do not set up any sectarian principles of their own, by which to shape and mould the proletarian movement . . . They always and everywhere represent the interests of the movement as a whole" ([1848] 1998: 50–1). The implication here is that the party and the class are one. They are in fact so in sync that the party need not "shape" or "mould" the workers' movement; all that is necessary is to "represent" the movement's interests. This presupposes (a) that the workers have one set of interests, and their bosses have another; (b) that those interests are collective and economic in character, and specifically those of two antagonistic social classes; and (c) that the proletariat's interests vis-à-vis their bosses are so self-evident that no other interpretation but that of the party's is possible.

The correspondence between party and class is just one axis along which party reflects society, however. With the second dimension, the Communist Party and the working class reflect "the history of all hitherto existing society," which for Marx and Engels is "the history of class struggles . . . Freeman and slave, patrician and plebeian, lord and serf, guild-master and journeyman, in a word, oppressor and oppressed" ([1848] 1998: 34–5). Referred to at turns as "historical" or "dialectical materialism," the Marxist philosophy of history holds that society is hurtling with increasing velocity from one class conflict to another, such that in present-day capitalist society, that conflict is simplifying into a massive and final antagonism. "Society as a whole is more and more splitting up into two great hostile camps," they write, "into two great classes directly facing each other: bourgeoisie and proletariat" ([1848] 1998: 35). Accordingly, the Communist Party and the workers' social movement are vehicles of the inexorable logic of history, which will resolve itself into a classless society through a Communist revolution, when the working class will seize the means of production from their bosses. In this sense, the Communists and the proletariat "merely express, in general terms, actual relations springing from an existing class struggle, from a historical movement going on under our very eyes" ([1848] 1998: 51).

The notion of the party as a reflection of society is repeated elsewhere in Marx's work, but as Tucker (1978) notes, Marx's *Contribution to the Critique of Political Economy* is "the *locus classicus* of historical materialism." It is in this piece, written some 11 years after the *Manifesto*, that Marx advances what has become known as the "economic determinist" or "base-superstructure" theory of politics and society. In the course of producing the necessities of life, Marx argues, "men enter into definite relations . . . relations of production" with other men. Depending on the society's "stage of development," those relations will vary as the *Manifesto* makes clear: under feudalism, the relations of production crystallize in the lord's exploitation of the serf; under slavery, the freeman's exploitation of the slave, and so on. In the *Contribution*, Marx refers to the "sum total of these relations" as "the economic structure of society, the real foundation." On top of the "real" world of production, Marx observes, "rises a legal and political superstructure and to which correspond definite forms of social consciousness. The mode of production of material life conditions the social, political and intellectual life process in general" ([1859] 1978: 4). If Marx and Engels viewed the party as the reflection of the working class, and the party and class in turn as the reflection of the class struggle, then in the *Contribution*, Marx stresses the importance of the socioeconomic even more. Here, politics and presumably the Communist Party are part of the "superstructure," which is only the surface-level manifestation of the more important economic "foundation" of social life. It is the social relations of production that "condition" political life, not the political that conditions the social. If a given party advances the policies it does, it is not because of its own internal dynamics, strategy, or motives, but rather because of the interests of the class or classes it represents.

The Marxist Reaction to Economic Determinism

Those who followed in Marx's footsteps became concerned with formulating socialist strategy in contexts that Marx had not yet encountered or did not expect. These contexts include early-twentieth-century Russia, a largely agricultural society where capitalism had not yet fully developed but where the socialist revolution succeeded, and Western Europe, where capitalism had flowered but where the socialist revolution had been repeatedly defeated. The observers examined here are therefore "Marxist" in the sense that they are broadly committed to Karl Marx's original project of emancipating the working class, but they are "unorthodox" in their Marxism because they sought to – or perhaps *had* to – re-read Marx to explain their particular historical and political context. Their work was not wholly without precedent in Marx's own writing. Many of them drew inspiration from a less well-known piece by Marx called *The Eighteenth Brumaire of Louis Bonaparte*. In this piece, arguably more than any other, Marx argues that politics play a role that is autonomous from, and therefore not merely a reflection of, the economic base of society.

The *Eighteenth Brumaire* is about the failure of the 1848 working-class revolution in France and the corresponding rise of conservative forces led by Napoleon's nephew, Louis, and supported by the French peasantry. Marx held that this outcome was not a question of economics, but of political strategy. Louis Napoleon was able to win the support of the peasants, Marx argues, by reminding them that it was his uncle who had freed them from feudalism. Moreover, Louis made sure to win the allegiance of the French military (Marx says, by feeding them "sausages") and thus neutralized a potential threat to his power. By contrast, the socialist party did neither of these things. They were unable, or perhaps did not think, to forge an urban–rural alliance, nor did they "smash" the state, which, with its military power and other resources, remained in place to shield the propertied classes from challenge ([1852] 1992: 236–9).

Since the autonomy of the political had a basis in Marx, his descendants turned their criticism against the most vocal spokesperson of economic determinism, Karl Kautsky, whose book, *The Class Struggle*, was the bible of the German Social Democratic Party (SPD) and the international workingman's party, the Second International. Kautsky predicted that the relentless advance of monopoly capitalism (or if you like, "big business") would destroy smaller capitalists, further swell the ranks of the working class, and lead inexorably to a revolutionary conflict. Thus, the 1891 program of the SPD reads, "Along with this monopolizing of the means of production goes the crowding out and scattering of small production . . . For the proletariat and the disappearing middle class – the small business men and farmers – it means increasing uncertainty in subsistence" (Kautsky 1910: 8). This system, Kautsky adds, "will finally lead to such unbearable conditions for the mass of the population that they will have no choice but to go down into degradation or to overthrow the system of private property" (Kautsky 1910: 90). For Kautsky, then, working-class revolution would occur *spontaneously* as an inevitable result of *economic* development. But if this were true, then to some Marxists, it became unclear what role, if any, socialist parties had in bringing about the revolution.

In his pamphlet *What is to be Done?* Vladimir Lenin (1902), the leader of the Russian Communist Party and Bolshevik Revolution, criticized economic determinism[3] as vulgar "spontaneism" and "economism." What economic determinists failed to grasp, according to Lenin, was that "with *all* the local organizations lacking a *single*, common, regular task" the working class could not hope, nor would they know how, to mount and sustain a revolutionary movement. A centralized "vanguard party" was necessary, for example, to publish a newspaper that could update workers on the latest injustices; time and coordinate armed insurrection when and where the state was weakest; and survive the authorities' successive attempts to arrest party leaders and thereby destroy or slow the momentum of the revolution. In this, Lenin was really the first Marxist to conceptualize the role of the party as something other than reflective of social divisions and mass struggles (Lenin [1902] 1973: 218–19).

Antonio Gramsci, the General Secretary of the Italian Communist

Party (PCI) in the 1920s, was deeply influenced by Lenin but moved beyond the latter's emphasis on party organization to focus on the problem of coalition-building.[4] Echoing the *Eighteenth Brumaire*, Gramsci argued that the central task of the PCI was, on the one hand, to convince the workers that they were the rightful leaders of Italian society, and, on the other, to forge an alliance with the peasantry against the rich. Together these two groups would comprise the PCI's majority coalition, or as Gramsci put it, its "hegemonic bloc." Thus, Gramsci writes that the PCI "made the urban proletariat the modern protagonist of Italian history," and in doing so "succeeded in modifying – if not completely at least to a notable extent – their mental outlook" ([1926] 1992: 48–9). But if the party convinces one group of their right to rule, then it must also organize other groups to consent *to be* ruled. To accomplish this difficult task, Gramsci hints that the PCI must frame competing political alternatives as impossible choices. For example, in Sardinia (an island off the west coast of Italy), the PCI organized the peasants to reject a local party's proposal to separate from the mainland in this way:

> Are you poor devils from Sardinia for a bloc with the gentry of the island, who have ruined you and who are the local overseers of capitalist exploitation? Or are you for a bloc with the revolutionary workers of the mainland, who want to destroy all forms of exploitation and free all the oppressed? ([1926] 1992: 34)

As Gramsci tells it, the PCI was able to win over the peasants by dividing Sardinians into antagonistic social classes. A bloc with the "gentry of the island" is said to be an unspeakable partnership with their hated "overseers," whereas a bloc with the "revolutionary workers of the mainland" is described as an opportunity to free themselves and "all of the oppressed."

The task of the party is therefore to organize subordinated groups such that they view as "common sense" that (a) society is divided into inimical social classes; (b) these social classes are the bourgeoisie and proletariat; and (c) the proletariat by rights should rule in place of the bourgeoisie. The party must work to define society in this way, because its political adversaries are attempting to organize alternative coalitions based on, say, religious divisions. Accordingly, Gramsci cautions, "Politically, the broad masses only exist insofar as they are organized within political parties" ([1921] 2000: 121). If for political constructionists the interests of racial groups have no objective existence unless parties mobilize the people along racial lines, then for Gramsci neither do the "broad masses." Workers and peasants must take for granted that they are indeed the subjugated multitude, but without a political party, they are not likely to come to that conclusion. "Ideas and opinions are not spontaneously 'born' in each individual brain," Gramsci insists, adding, "they have a centre of formation, of irradiation, of dissemination, of persuasion – a group of men . . . which has developed them and presented them in the political form of current reality" (1971: 192). By addressing the relationship between party and society in this way, Gramsci famously turned the base-superstructure model on its head. Political struggle did not reflect the structural antagonism of owning and non-owning classes (i.e., the relations of production). Rather class antagonism reflected the content of political struggle.

The process by which subordinated groups come to see themselves as classes is similar in Louis Althusser, whose work is sometimes associated with Gramsci's. For Althusser, the survival of capitalism depends not only on the repressive state apparatus (e.g., the power of the military), but also on "ideological state apparatuses" (ISAs) like schools, news organizations, parties, and churches, which obtain the cooperation of the people through "interpellation." Interpellation is the process by which individuals recognize themselves as concrete "subjects," that is, as persons having a meaningful identity or place in society. Thus, Althusser observes,

> Ideology "acts" or "functions" in such a way that it "recruits" subjects among the individuals . . . or "transforms" the individuals into subjects . . . by that very precise operation which I have called *interpellation* or hailing, and which can be imagined along the lines of the most commonplace everyday police (or other) hailing: "Hey, you

there!" ... the hailed individual will turn round. By this mere one-hundred-and-eighty-degree physical conversion, he becomes a *subject*. Why? Because he has recognized that the hail was "really" addressed to him, and "it was *really him* who was hailed." (Althusser [1970] 2001: 174; emphasis in original)

Interpellation is a necessary part of preserving the capitalist order because of the variety of identities one can embrace. An individual may be "hailed" as a "boy or girl" or "a worker, a boss or a soldier" (Althusser [1970] 2001: 176, 178). Provided that workers are hailed by their community's ISAs as patriots, white people, or any number of other non-class subjectivities, and provided that workers then "recognize" themselves in the call (i.e., they turn around and say, "Yes?"), then it is unlikely that workers will spontaneously recognize themselves as a revolutionary class. For Althusser, it is parties and other ISAs that organize people to see themselves as members of non-class collectives. Put another way, the capitalist system will survive so long as parties and other ISAs are able to make people think of themselves as anything other than antagonistic social classes.

The Neo-Gramscians

Broadly speaking, the neo-Gramscian view of the exclusive party is anchored in their namesake's rejection of economic determinism. Among the earliest pieces in the neo-Gramscian tradition is Adam Przeworski's (1977) reappraisal of Kautsky's *The Class Struggle*.[5] Because Kautsky and other orthodox Marxists had assumed that classes formed naturally among those who shared the same position in the world of factory production (e.g., workers, factory owners), Przeworski was particularly concerned with the problem of organizing the unemployed, who had no productive employment and therefore fell outside Marxist theories of class formation (1977: 344).

Przeworski's solution was to insist, as Gramsci did, that people coalesced into classes because of political struggles, not because of their relationship to the means of production. Thus, Przeworski writes, "*Classes are not given uniquely by any objective positions because they constitute effects of struggles*" (1977: 367; emphasis in original). But if classes are the effects of struggles, and if therefore the unemployed will only see themselves as part of the working class if they are organized as workers, then presumably they may be organized in other ways. That is, if socialists do not take this problem seriously, then they may be in danger of being out-organized by competing political parties, who will want the unemployed to embrace alternative identities and perhaps even to blame socialists for their joblessness. The challenge and necessity of political struggle, then, lies in the fact that "social cleavages, the experience of social differentiation, are never given directly to our consciousness. Social differences acquire the status of cleavages as an outcome of ideological and political struggles" (Przeworski 1977: 370).

Furthermore, it is not enough for political parties to name social divisions; divisions are part of larger visions that parties must articulate of what society is and ought to be. "Parties," he argues, "participate in the process of class formation in the course of struggles that fundamentally concern the very vision of society." That vision consists of answers to basic questions about society such as:

> Is the society composed of classes or of individuals with harmonious interests? Are classes the fundamental source of social cleavage or are they to be placed alongside any other social distinction? Are interests of classes antagonistic or do they encourage cooperation? What are the classes? Which class represents interests more general than its own? Which constitute a majority? Which are capable of leading the entire society?

Far from being able to assume that the poor will naturally support socialist or labor parties, Marxists must formulate and vocalize their answers to these fundamental questions of vision, and thereby organize the unemployed to see themselves as one with the poor and subjugated masses and against the rich. Put simply, "The ideological struggle is a struggle *about* class before it is a struggle *among* classes" (1977: 371; emphasis in original).

Przeworski and Sprague's (1986) *Paper Stones* is essentially a reapplication of the foregoing theoretical framework to voting. In contrast to the voter-centered theories in the first half of this book, which assume that voters make their choices based on loyalty to social group, familial partisanship, or rational interest, the authors argue, as Przeworski did in 1977, that "the voting behavior of individuals is an effect of the activities of political parties." To understand why voters make the choices they do, we must, on their account, examine "the cumulative consequence of the strategies pursued by political parties," especially of the Left. This is partly because socialist parties are faced with one of the most important dilemmas in western politics, namely, how to win a majority when their working-class base is a minority of the electorate. Socialist parties must, in other words, choose between remaining ideologically pure but indefinitely in opposition, on the one hand, and diluting Marxist principles but in doing so have a chance to govern, on the other. How voters vote depends principally on whether socialist parties are on the scene, and if so, on how those parties resolve the "dilemma of electoral socialism." Accordingly, they write, "this study is a study of voting, but not of voters" (1986: 3–4, 10–11).

If for Przeworski the next frontier in socialist strategy is to expand the meaning of the working class to include the unemployed, then for Laclau and Mouffe it is to move beyond class and advance a new political project that can unite the "struggles against sexism, racism, sexual discrimination, and in the defense of the environment" with the struggles of workers ([1985] 2001: xviii, 134). The unification of these seemingly disparate groups is possible for precisely the same reason that Przeworski fears the organization of the unemployed by political adversaries, namely, that interests and identities are never given and may therefore be articulated together in grand left- (or right-)wing coalitions. Their "central argument," they emphasize, is that "social antagonisms are not objective relations; the political is not superstructure." They add, "Politics ... does not consist in simply registering already existing interests but plays a crucial role in shaping political subjects" ([1985] 2001: xiii–xiv, xvii).

In this, Laclau and Mouffe recuperate Gramsci's focus on organizing hegemonic coalitions or blocs, but incorporate Althusser's concept of interpellation by suggesting that socialists are actually creating "political subjects" when they bring people together. Unlike Althusser, however, Laclau and Mouffe hold that political organizations need not hail subjects with singular identities such as "woman" or "worker," but may construct a multidimensional "chain of equivalences," in which a party might hail "anti-racist – feminist – anti-homophobic – Green – trade unionist" subjects. Conversely, such a hailing would demonize their adversaries as "racist – sexist – homophobic – global warming denialist – millionaires" ([1985] 2001: xviii).

Laclau and Mouffe insist that it is not sufficient to define an "us and them," however. Powerful chains of equivalences take hold when political organizations articulate an overarching vision of the kind of society "we" want to be. Thus, they conclude their preface to the second edition of *Hegemony and Socialist Strategy* by saying, "If one is to build a chain of equivalences among democratic struggles, one needs to establish a frontier and define an adversary, but this is not enough. One also needs to know for what one is fighting, what kind of society one wants to establish" [1985] 2001: xix).

By now, all of these Marxists must seem indistinguishable from each other, so by way of prelude to the last perspective in this section, it may be helpful to take stock by flagging the differences among them. The *Eighteenth Brumaire* is a somewhat thin reed upon which to build an alternative Marxist interpretation of party and society. Marx's instructions to the working class to form an alliance with the peasantry and smash the state offer a hint that political strategy may be more important than he had originally let on, but he does not actually explain the relationship between party and society. Indeed, party politics as such are really peripheral to Marx's analysis in that piece. This is to say nothing of the fact that he is much clearer about that relationship in the *Manifesto* and *Contribution* except that those pieces directly contradict the *Eighteenth Brumaire*.

Lenin and Gramsci agree broadly that parties divide society into antagonistic groups, but they diverge from each other in two ways. First, as Gramsci is careful to point out, a direct frontal assault on the state such as the one Lenin advocates in *What is to be Done?* is possible only when the ruling class has no base of support in civil society and thus is unable to furnish an outer defense for the state. Italy and the European powers were different from Russia, Gramsci argued, because the ruling classes in those countries controlled a robust network of civic institutions (e.g., the Catholic Church) that worked to prevent revolutionary class consciousness from taking hold. The second difference proceeds from the first, for whereas Lenin's emphasis was on building a disciplined and ubiquitous party organization that could smash the state, Gramsci's focus in Italy was on cultivating "organic intellectuals" among the working class who could help infiltrate civil society and in doing so forge a coalition of workers and peasants.

I have hinted that Althusser and Gramsci are similar to each other because of the importance of workers' recognition of class divisions to acquiring and maintaining political power. However, Althusser's concept of interpellation is closer to "identification," whereas Gramsci's accent in the concept of the hegemonic bloc is on coalition building and acquiring the *consent* of lesser partners to be ruled by the working class. Put another way, for Gramsci the lesser partner "kneels," while for Althusser the subject "turns around" in recognition of his identity.

Finally, it bears mention that if the party is the pivotal actor in the thought of Lenin, Gramsci, and Przeworski, then for Althusser and Laclau and Mouffe, it is less so. Parties comprise only one of several possible ideological state apparatuses in Althusser. In Laclau and Mouffe, parties are shadows and are only ever implied by their frequent references to "politics" and "articulation."

It is within the development of the Marxist tradition that de Leon et al. (2009) must be understood. Their critique of the notion that parties reflect society is that it assumes an "elective affinity" or natural fit between certain historical conjunctures (e.g., economic crises) and certain cleavages (e.g., class). For example, in the *Manifesto*, Marx and Engels suggest that the bourgeois-proletarian divide is an artifact of the rise of capitalism. Yet in the present day, which is also a time of widespread economic deprivation, the cleavages that have emerged are non-economic in character. Thus, de Leon et al. seek to explain the ascendancy of Hindu nationalism in India, Islamism in Turkey, and colorblind racism in the United States. The principal problem with orthodox Marxism, as with any crude social determinism (e.g., Lazarsfeld et al. [1944] 1948) for that matter, is that it cannot explain why one cleavage (e.g., religion) becomes important politically, while another, which is equally salient (e.g., class), does not.

For example, according to the 2001 Census of India, 80.5 percent of Indians are ethnically Hindu, yet for most of the years since India's independence from the British empire in 1947, the ruling party has not been the Hindu nationalist Bharatiya Janata Party (BJP), but rather the Congress Party. Indeed, the first BJP prime minister was elected in 1998. Prior to that moment, Hindu identity had not been an especially salient political cleavage. Scholars and other commentators have sought to explain the BJP's late appeal as largely the result of social factors such as the rise of the middle classes, the growing political importance of the lower castes, and rapid socioeconomic change since the breakdown of state socialism. But none of these explains why a Hindu bloc in a majority Hindu country had taken so long to materialize, especially given the fact that the BJP has roots going back to the 1950s. Manali Desai argues that for much of the post-independence era, the Congress and Communist parties were able to suppress the religious cleavage in favor of others such as caste and class. Conversely, the BJP's ascendancy was at least partly due to its own practices: through violent protest and other tactics, the BJP was at last able to frame Hindus as a victimized constituency and the Congress Party as "corrupt, westernized and elitist" (Census of India 2011; de Leon et al. 2009: 204).

Thus, de Leon et al.'s solution to the problem of "why this cleavage, but not that one?" is to suggest that political parties articulate "the social" in their struggle for power. This is called "political articulation," defined as the process through which *party practices naturalize class, ethnic, and racial formations as a basis of social division by integrating disparate interests and identities*

149

into coherent sociopolitical blocs" (de Leon et al. 2009: 194–5; emphasis in original). This definition may be broken down into three parts. To begin, parties make divisions such as class, race, and religion *seem* natural or real. This dovetails with much of the exclusive party approach, which assumes that social cleavages only become salient when parties make them a focal point. Next, parties go through the trouble of making these fictive divisions seem real, because victory depends on the parties' ability to construct a majority bloc; that is, to frame their own supporters as the natural majority who should rule and their opponents' supporters as the minority who shouldn't. But third, political articulation is about more than just cleavages and elections. Of course, there are parties that are concerned only with winning campaigns, but de Leon et al. have in mind creative or ethical parties that, in articulating "the social," are attempting to bring an entire social order into being such as a theocracy, a worker's republic, or an unregulated free market society.

Political articulation is therefore an improvement on existing Marxist approaches to party and society in two ways. First, it recognizes the importance of socioeconomic change without being economically deterministic. Moments of crisis are said to expand the universe of possible alternative cleavages along which to reorganize society. In this, de Leon et al. do not propose a voluntaristic theory: parties cannot articulate new cleavages at will. That said, while socioeconomic change is important, *how* it is important politically is shaped by competing parties. In the absence of any major disruption, there is little room for parties to advance a new way for people to see themselves as different from one another. However, once a disruption does take place, the disruption itself cannot determine which social divisions will become important and which will recede into the background. That gets decided in the arena of partisan struggle. For example, a recession has no natural political valence or meaning: liberals, conservatives, socialists, and Neo-Nazis may use a recession to organize people in radically different directions.

Secondly, the political articulation framework reasserts the central role of the party without assuming (as Gramsci does) that political parties are primarily concerned with organizing classes. de Leon et al. thereby retain the openness of Laclau and Mouffe to alternative cleavages while not going as far as to imply that just any organization may accomplish articulation. Though parties are not the only groups that organize whole societies, parties are better positioned than others to organize people into competing blocs and to propose alternative chains of equivalences.

I end this section with a related set of works consisting of neo-Gramscian forays into debates beyond Marxism, especially on the origins of political "moderation" in democratic societies and transitions to democracy, modernity, and capitalism. An important early exemplar of this work is Riley and Desai's (2007) article on passive revolution in India and Italy. "Passive revolution" was a term used by Gramsci for cases in which political parties press revolutionary rhetoric and tactics into the service of conservative projects. Passive revolutions may be violent or non-violent, Riley and Desai say, depending on the timing of nationhood and lower class mobilization. Because the anti-colonial struggle in India occurred at the same time as mass mobilization, elites, who comprised the leadership of the Congress Party, were able to recruit the lower classes to the cause of independence from Britain in a way that left their perch at the top of Indian society unchallenged. By contrast, in Italy, mass mobilization reached its height between the First and Second World Wars, well after Italian unification (in 1870), and was often antagonistic towards elites. This led the latter to support the violent repression of workers and peasants at the hands of the Fascist Party. Similarly, de Leon (2008) argues that the American route to liberal democracy was made possible by the Republican Party, which he calls a "bourgeois mass party." In the absence of such an organization, he argues, the Northeast–Midwest coalition that prosecuted the war against the slave South would have been unlikely. Further, although the U.S. Civil War was revolutionary to the degree that it ended slavery, it was also conservative in the sense that any criticism of capitalism after the North's victory was violently repressed. Finally, Tuğal (2009), in his own interpretation of passive revolution, critiques the popular assumption that Islamism poses a challenge to Western style neoliberalism or "globalization." On the contrary, he argues, the Islamist AKP in Turkey has used revolutionary religious rhetoric opportunistically to absorb the challenge of Islamist radicals and in doing so has managed to inaugurate rather than subvert neoliberalization.

This work has at least two important implications. First, unlike much of the transitions literature, which stresses the role of social classes in bringing about modernization, democratization, and capitalism, neo-Gramscians foreground the role of political parties in those processes. Second, unlike moderation theory, which holds that radicals who participate in democratic politics will moderate their views (and conversely that radicals who are excluded will become more radical), neo-Gramscians insist that moderation is not made inevitable by democratic participation and depends on a host of factors, not least of which is internal party strategy. The result, as in the case of the Italian Fascist Party, may be anything but moderate. [6]

Important Reactions within Marxism: A Qualified Reassertion of Class over Party

Michael Burawoy, in an important essay published in 1989, criticized both orthodox Marxism on the one hand, and Przeworski's party-centered analysis on the other. If orthodox Marxism's fatal conceit is that workers forge their identities automatically based on "macro-factors" such as a society's stage of economic development, then in Burawoy's view, Przeworski makes a similar mistake by claiming that workers' identities originate in another abstract macro-factor, namely, electoral politics. "Przeworski's critique," he writes, "lacks precisely what orthodoxy lacks – micro-foundations," which are "grounded in production and the lived experience it generates" among workers, especially in the context of the workplace. As such, parties can only ever be in a position to translate and take into account those identities in the realm of politics. The truth of this, he notes, lies in the fact that in non-democratic societies, "the absence of electoral competition between parties . . . does not prevent workers from developing a class understanding of their society" (Burawoy 1989: 82–5).

Those who are familiar with Ron Aminzade's (1993) work on the Republican Party and working-class formation in France may be surprised that his book, *Ballots and Barricades*, is not featured in the main body of this chapter. But, like Burawoy, he is critical of both orthodox class analysts and those who proclaim the autonomy of the political. Seeking to explain why mid-nineteenth-century French workers in some cities took to the ballot box, while others took to the barricades, he finds, contrary to orthodox Marxism, that levels of industrialization did not correspond well to worker activism. Cities like Rouen, which experienced the rapid rise of factory production, did not field the most politically active or radical workers. Conversely, cities like Toulouse, which were economic backwaters, produced the most militant revolutionaries. Aminzade argues that these divergent outcomes depended partly on whether or not liberals, radicals, or socialists controlled the local Republican Party. However, he is also quick to point out that parties do not just divide workers at will. The relevance of parties is constrained by two important social factors. Workers' structural position in the realm of production – that is, their class position – defines the constellation of potential interests that parties can draw upon in their appeal for support. For instance, a politician cannot appeal to relatively prosperous artisans by railing against the back-breaking, gut-wrenching poverty of the working class. Such a message would fall flat, because that is not the class position that these particular workers occupy. Furthermore, the ability of parties to "create identities independent of workplace relations . . . varies over time and place." For example, "periods of rapid social and political change" like mid-nineteenth-century France provide more opportunities for parties to forge alternative social identities. Accordingly, Aminzade refers to his approach, not as a party-centered analysis, but "a non-reductionist *class* analysis" (Aminzade 1993: 4–9, 13, 252; emphasis added).

*

We end as always and for the last time with the main arguments of the book. The first argument is that the literature on democratic party politics will be misunderstood without a knowledge of sociology's place within it. For instance, an important debate in this chapter concerns the assumption that political actors are self-interested utility-maximizing individuals. Had our map of the field been confined to the dominant voter-centered approaches, we might have thought that the only objection to rational choice theory was the Michigan model's contention that voters are actually not that rational at all (see pp. 40–1). We might have assumed further that the main combatants in the rationality debate were economists, political scientists, and social psychologists. As it turns out, sociologists have been rather active in questioning the givenness of interests, and their main tack in doing so has not been to expose the irrationality of the average voter (the polarization debates in chapter 2, pp. 44–6, notwithstanding), but to highlight the ways in which partisan contention naturalizes interests.

This fact bears on my next argument, namely that sociological approaches are not reducible to the Columbia model. Chapters 1 and 6 may be read as offering opposite approaches: where the Columbia model assumes that social cleavages precede and therefore condition partisan struggle (see pp. 21–2), the scholars in this chapter (legislative coalitions excepted) argue that political parties construct or articulate social cleavages. Additionally, it is no exaggeration to say that Marxism was the nemesis of many a scholar of political parties. Indeed, power elite theory was taken (incorrectly) to be synonymous with Marxism, a notion that emboldened the pluralist reaction and injected the flavor of the Cold War into some of the debates reviewed in this book (see pp. 102, 114–16). That Marxism loomed large as an intellectual "other" furnishes additional evidence that sociology cannot be reduced to the work of Lazarsfeld and Berelson, who were accepted as mainstream.

My third argument is that a turf war between the disciplines would shed more heat than light. Although it is important to know that rational actor theories are less prevalent in sociology than in other social sciences, nevertheless, the sociologists and political scientists in this chapter share the view that the distinguishing feature of parties is their exclusiveness. Further, the proponents of the Michigan model, who were social psychologists and political scientists, have in common with constructivists and Marxists a skepticism of models based on individual rationality.

Fourthly, I have written that voter- and party-centered approaches are not in conversation with each other. Though I maintain that Lipset was the only major theorist to bridge this divide by championing the functional party and social voter approaches simultaneously (see p. 23), it bears mention that constructivists and neo-Gramscian Marxists are at least explicitly critical of the Columbia model's assumption that social cleavages exist independently of partisan struggle. Accordingly, we find in this chapter something approaching another exception to the argument that the two great wings of the literature are self-referential.

My fifth claim is that much of the field assumes an impermeable boundary around party that separates it from the state and civil society. This assumption, I have said, appears to contradict how parties behave in practice. Like other party-centered approaches, the exclusive party is less guilty of this charge than its voter-centered counterparts. The state is theorized in at least four ways in this chapter. The first two center on party–state relations. In the legislative coalition tradition, the state reserves to itself the prerogatives of patronage and public policy, and it is these powers that legislators seek when they form parties. In Slez and Martin's institutionalist account, both state and party formation are artifacts of the questions settled in the constitutional phase of American democratization. States and parties take further shape as they confront the issues still left on the table. Marxism supplies the next two theories of the state, but, unlike most approaches in this book, they address the intersection of party, state, and society head-on.[7] Within the logic of orthodox Marxism, party and state are mere superstructure and are therefore reducible to class relations. That is, one can understand the policies enacted by states and parties simply by understanding the balance of class power in a given society. For example, a strong welfare state and socialist party are indications that workers are in the ascendant, whereas a laissez-faire (i.e., unregulated, free market) state and a strong conservative party are indications that capitalists are on the rise. Another Marxist theory of the state that is at least implicit in this book is Gramsci's. For him, the balance of power is not just between classes, but also between the state and civil society. State power is one of domination and is therefore dependent on the coercive military and police apparatus for its enactment. The revolutionary party should only engage in a full frontal assault on the state (i.e., a violent war of maneuver) under two conditions: when the state is weak and the bourgeoisie have a tenuous hold on civil society. If the state is weak, but the masses remain convinced that the bourgeoisie should rule or that a free market capitalist economy is the best of all worlds, then a revolutionary party would do well to first infiltrate the key institutions of civil society (e.g., schools, churches, the media) in a battle for hearts and minds before attempting a violent insurrection. In sum, whereas orthodox Marxism's solution to the intersection of party, state, and society is to suggest that state and party reflect the balance of class power, Gramsci's solution is to add that the balance of power between the state and civil society is regulated by parties in struggle.

7

Party, State, and Society

This book might fruitfully be summed up in two interrelated analytical moves. The first has been to remap the scholarship on democratic party politics to include the diversity of sociological approaches beyond the Columbia model. But in joining the work of sociologists to that of other social scientists, the book also contends that the revised map points to new and better explanations for the ways in which political parties intersect with civil society and the state.

The most robust early solutions to the problem of intersectionality – all from the second half of this book – are the Michelsian, the functionalist, and the Marxist. To repeat, in the Iron Rule tradition, parties begin as the representatives of allied social movements, only to become absorbed in the pursuit of state power. Thus, the Michelsian story is really about the transition from a party-movement to a state-party (see p. 102). Taken together, the various traditions of the functional approach amount to one claim, namely, that political parties mediate between civil society and the state. In the absence of parties, democratic states would be paralyzed by constitutional checks and balances, while social conflicts would erupt regularly in revolution or some other form of instability (see p. 123). Marxism supplies at least two solutions. Within orthodox Marxism, parties and the state reflect the balance of class power in society. The Gramscian solution, by contrast, confers more autonomy on parties and the state but is essentially a theory of revolutionary strategy. Where the state and bourgeois civil society are weak, it is appropriate for socialist parties to attempt a violent overthrow of the state; where bourgeois civil society is strong, socialist parties should first undertake a campaign of persuasion and quiet infiltration (see pp. 155–6).

Though these earlier works go some way toward explaining more recent cases of intersectionality, the fit between classical theory and contemporary practice is somewhat awkward, owing to the fluid continuum in which some of today's parties stand in relation to states and social movements. In the most extreme cases, which I call omnibus parties, it is difficult to discern where the party begins and where it ends.

Consider the cases of Hamas and Hezbollah. Before winning formal state power, both organizations provided vital social services to marginalized communities (e.g., Shiite Muslims in the southern suburbs of Beirut). For example, in Lebanon, Hezbollah was a "state within a state": it built and maintained homes, roads, and wells, ran hospitals and schools, and provided jobs and financial assistance to the poor (Azani 2009: 71–2; Gunning 2008: 45, 254–5; Hroub 2010: 68–70; Jaber 1997: 147; Roy 2011: 100–2; Van Engeland 2008a: 38–9). In this sense, each organization was a social movement acting as a parallel welfare state to the actual state. Building their base in this way, Hamas and Hezbollah then became institutionalized political parties. Eventually, each party was able to leverage the mass support built through the provision of social services to win elections and exercise sovereignty over their respective territories: Hamas in Gaza, Hezbollah in Southern Lebanon (Azani 2009: 232, 239; Hroub 2010: 151, 162–5; Roy 2011: 206–14; Van Engeland 2008a: 47). Beyond acting as a parallel state, then, the two movement parties found themselves in the position of enacting formal state power. Thus, Hamas shocked the world by winning the Palestinian legislative elections of 2006 and then outflanked international forces seeking to depose them (e.g., Israel, the United States) with a military takeover of Gaza in June 2007 (Hroub 2010: xxiv–xxv; Roy 2011: 213–14). Furthermore, it bears mention that Hamas and Hezbollah are not isolated from one another: together with the Muslim Brotherhood, another movement party that found itself in power in Egypt, they formed an *alliance* of omnibus parties that crossed national borders.

The African National Congress (ANC) in South Africa is still another case in point. A nationalist movement of non-violent resistance from its founding in 1912 through the 1950s, the ANC formed a military arm called Umkhonto in the 1960s after the apartheid state's infamous massacre of protesters at Sharpeville. Though literally hundreds of organizations comprised the South African liberation struggle and though its insurrectionary activities were largely stifled by the apartheid security apparatus, Umkhonto's position at the forefront of the armed resistance helped to establish the ANC as the movement's natural leader. Accordingly, by the 1980s, when the apartheid state and liberation movement had reached a stalemate and begun a negotiated democratic transition, the ANC emerged as the natural "government in waiting." Moreover, throughout this process, the ANC, acting very much like a state already, conducted a dazzling diplomatic strategy that had governments all over the world imposing sanctions on South Africa to end apartheid. Eventually, having evolved into a formidable political party with an elaborate organizational structure and a mass base, the ANC won 62.7 percent of the popular vote in the 1994 legislative elections, carrying at least one third of the votes in every province. Today, the ANC remains the only truly national party in South Africa and is that country's undisputed ruling regime (Marais 2011: 13–76; Van Engeland 2008b).

What is needed to account for omnibus parties like the ANC is a delicate balance of fluidity and autonomy: a recognition that parties may be permeable to states and social movements without being altogether reducible to them. The following works are featured below, because they are to my knowledge the closest we have come in recent years to striking this balance. As we shall see, each falls short in one particular or another. The cartel party thesis successfully captures the intersection of state and party but like Michels assumes a disconnect with civil society (see p. 102). Cultural approaches bring together party, state, and society but fall somewhat short of the fluidity that is characteristic of omnibus parties. Finally, movement-based approaches and synthetic approaches to symbolic and exclusive politics blur the boundary between party and society but largely sidestep the role of the state.

Across the Divide: Symbolic and Exclusive Politics

Voter- and party-centered approaches are isolated from one another as I have said repeatedly, but they need not be. For example, the partisan voter and exclusive party are complementary concepts. Recall that for constructivists and Marxists, parties build majority coalitions by persuading potential constituents that their society is organized in one way and not another (see pp. 124–5). To merge this insight with those of symbolic politics and information processing (see pp. 47–55), one might suggest that to naturalize social cleavages, political parties must trigger affective associations that are linked to early life: the party cannot divide and conquer unless it proposes lines of cleavage that resonate with people emotionally. Some existing work already gestures in this direction. Alvarez and Nagler (2004), Baldassari and Gelman (2008), Carmines and Stimson (1989), and Zaller (1992), for instance, all suggest that party polarization affects public opinion.

Critiques of mass society accomplish the same synthesis but with a healthy dose of Michelsian skepticism. A canonical work in this area is Edelman's ([1964] 1974) *The Symbolic Uses of Politics*, which holds that parties use emotionally charged symbols to secure the acquiescence of the mass public. "Political symbols," Edelman writes, "bring out in concentrated form those particular meanings and emotions which members of a group create and reinforce in each other," such that "Language becomes a sequence of Pavlovian cues rather than an instrument for reasoning and analysis if situation and appropriate cue occur together" ([1964] 1974: 11–12, 116). Steven Schier's (2000) work on "activation" is a more recent entry in this genre. Parties, Schier says, have de-emphasized mobilizing voters in favor of broadcasting political symbols via direct mail and television ads that "activate" or "microtarget" key voting blocs on election day without truly involving them in the democratic process.

The Cartel Party Thesis: a Neo-Michelsian Strategy

A second solution to the problem of intersectionality is Katz and Mair's "cartel party thesis" (Katz and Mair 1995, 2009). Their argument is that "political parties increasingly function like cartels, employing the resources of the state to limit political competition and ensure their own electoral success." Cartelization, they write, was partly a response to certain large-scale social transformations. One was the decline of class politics described above by Inglehart (1990) (see p. 25), which swept away many of the partisan divisions of the immediate postwar period. Another was the steep increase in the costs of campaigning in the mass media – costs that the dues of party members simply could not meet. These challenges prompted parties to rely less on their constituents and more on what Katz and Mair call "state subventions," which include public financing for elections and the use of public service broadcasting for campaign publicity (Katz and Mair 2009: 753, 755).

The end result, they argue, has been the interpenetration of parties with the state and the widening disjuncture of party from society, a two-fold process that is yet another kind of Michelsian party oligarchy for the twenty-first century (see pp. 85–7). Evidence for the cartel party thesis includes the ideological homogenization of parties and the rise of "anti-party system" organizations that have emerged in reaction to the cartels. Concomitantly, because of the cooperation among parties to retain or gain access to state resources, parties no longer disagree on substantive policy issues – they argue instead over questions of technocratic expertise (i.e., who can manage the government most efficiently). In this, party labels are becoming less meaningful in some democratic polities than coalitions of parties such as the so-called "center-left" and "center-right" coalitions of Italy and other European states (Katz and Mair 2009: 759, 762).

Cultural Approaches to the State: Marxism Stretched

Cultural approaches to the state, some of which are inspired by Marxism, provide another fruitful entry point to the problem of intersectionality. Recall that for Weber the state "claims the *monopoly of the legitimate use of physical force* within a given territory" (Weber 1946: 78; emphasis in original). Weber's definition of the state is about sovereignty, and as such tells us that "society" consists of those "within a given territory" who do not possess sufficient means of coercion to challenge the state's ultimate authority. Cultural approaches challenge the Weberian assumption that the state is a solid entity, separate and distinct from society. Philip Abrams once wrote that in studying the state it is critical to distinguish between the "state-system," which refers to institutionalized practices, and the "state-idea," which denotes the symbolic representation of that system as something real and possessing concrete characteristics (Abrams 1988: 82).

Similarly, Timothy Mitchell, in a now famous essay, argues that the appearance of the state as an autonomous actor is the "effect" of "methods of organization, arrangement, and representation," which draw lines of distinction that are in practice not there (Mitchell 1999: 77–8). For example, the U.S. banking system comprises tightly interlocking relationships between major banks like Citibank, the semipublic Federal Reserve, the U.S. Treasury, and deposit insurance agencies like the Federal Deposit Insurance Corporation (FDIC). Additionally, public officials are often former banking executives and vice versa. Before serving as Treasury Secretary under President George W. Bush, for instance, Henry Paulson had been CEO of Goldman Sachs. Demarcating where the state ends and society begins is exceedingly difficult, yet, Mitchell observes, bankers and government officials are careful to insist that they are separate from one another. Why the immense investment in maintaining a bright line that is in practice a revolving door? For Mitchell, "producing and maintaining the distinction between state and society is itself a mechanism that generates resources and power" and through which "a certain social and political order is maintained" (Mitchell 1999: 83). For instance, to perpetuate the image of a democratic society, government officials must through rhetoric and other practices such as "regulation" insinuate that it does not collude with the rich at the expense of middle- and lower-income citizens. Meanwhile bankers must keep up the appearance that they do not exercise undue influence on government officials.

Parties may be implicated in this process if we assume that at least some of the people who are responsible for maintaining the powerful state-society distinction are members of political parties. The work of Bob Jessop in *State Theory* suggests how this can be accomplished. He writes that the "the unity of the state" is itself a "project." Following the articulatory role of political parties in Gramsci, he writes that the promotion of party spirit gives shape and coherence to the state and links it to the national popular imagination by framing it in particular ways, for example, as an ally, an enemy, an enforcer, or an arbiter (Jessop 1990: 364). If party, state, and society are more intertwined than previously thought, then for Jessop it is because political parties may frame the state as separate from, or more integrated with, civil society.

Movement-Based Strategies

A field of inquiry that has been engaged for some time in addressing the problem of intersectionality is the social movement literature, though solutions differ from one analyst to the next. One solution has been to blur as much as possible the line between movements and parties. Referring to sociology's near monopoly over the study of social movements, and political science's corresponding corner on political parties, Burstein (1998), for example, writes, "It is not that sociologists and political scientists are studying different things that could usefully be combined; rather, they are studying the same thing without realizing it" (1998: 47, 55). Similarly, Mildred Schwartz's concept of "party movements," otherwise known as third parties, refers to "organizations . . . that, no matter how radical their goals or how willing to use non-institutional means, are still prepared to work within the system like any political party because they see government office as the most direct way of achieving their objectives" (2006: 11). For her, party and movement are fused, because such organizations not only exhibit characteristics of both movements and parties, but also adopt "strategies of persistence" (i.e., faction, takeover, purge, merger, makeover, or abeyance) that may emphasize one organizational form or another over time as they struggle to survive (2006: 4–5, 44–6). A movement that is dissatisfied with politics-as-usual, may start out as a minority faction in an existing party, then take over the party as its dominant faction, and eventually lose its movement-like characteristics as it becomes exclusively preoccupied with mainstream electoral competition. Scholars of Latin American politics have made similar observations about indigenous movements, which do things that parties normally do like field political candidates (Pugh 2008; Yashar 2005).

Another solution may be found in Goldstone's 2003 edited volume, *States, Parties, and Social Movements*. In it, Goldstone and his collaborators challenge the claim that social movements occupy the sphere of non-institutional politics, whereas political parties comprise institutionalized politics or the political establishment. Against this assumption, the Goldstone volume holds that "social movements constitute an essential element of normal politics in modern societies" (Goldstone 2003: 1–2). Specifically, the essays in the book argue that social movements *"shape and give rise to* parties, courts, legislatures, and elections" and that "citizenship rights and political party systems are developing out of social movements" (Goldstone 2003: 2–3; emphasis added). Goldstone's overall vision is therefore one in which omnibus parties spring from social movements. Movements may become states (as in Glenn's chapter on the anticommunist movement in Czechoslovakia) or parties that win formal state power (as in Desai's chapter on the Communist Party in Kerala and Bengal, India).

If social movements are the starting point of party and state formation in the Goldstone volume, then in the *Dynamics of Contention* (2001, 2010) or DOC project inaugurated by McAdam, Tarrow, and Tilly, the relationship between parties and social movements is noticeably more dialogical and thus vaguely reminiscent of the functional approach's emphasis on mediating institutions (see p. 123). The DOC project arose in part out of a dissatisfaction with "single actor" and "movement-centric" accounts of complex social transformations such as democratization and revolution. In a 2010 retrospective piece on their efforts to overcome this limitation, McAdam and Tarrow write that one area in need of more careful study is the relationship between elections and social movements. Their approach to theorizing this intersection is to hypothesize six mechanisms that, in one combination or another, might link social movements to electoral dynamics in a given episode of contentious politics. "Transferable innovations" denote the methods that social movements invent but that parties then adopt in electoral campaigns. Here the authors make much of the 2008 Obama campaign's adoption of online recruitment techniques, pioneered by the post-9/11 U.S. antiwar movement. In "taking the electoral option," McAdam and Tarrow refer to cases in which movements become parties or "movement states" as they did in Nazi Germany and Fascist Italy. "Proactive electoral mobilization" points to spikes in activity that occur when movements perceive an opportunity or threat in an impending election. There is also a "reactive" variant of this that occurs *after* an election. "Movement/party polarization" is a spinoff of Zald and Berger's (1978) seminal claim that movements can form *within* parties and other organizations and tear them apart. For example, Democrats in the American South called "Dixiecrats" bolted their party in response to the growing influence of the Civil Rights Movement, while the movement, in turn, formed the "Mississippi Freedom Democratic Party" in a bid to unseat their state's all-white delegation at the 1964 Democratic National Convention. Finally, McAdam and Tarrow hold that the "oscillations of electoral regimes" (that is, shifts in dominance from one party to another) powerfully condition the prospects for successful mobilization. Thus, the Reagan administration (1981–9) facilitated the emergence of the Christian Right, militia, pro-life, and anti-immigrant movements in the United States (McAdam and Tarrow 2010: 529, 533–5).

*

Adjudicating among, and playing with, these more recent solutions to intersectionality is, in my view, the next step for students of democratic party politics, but we cannot take it unless we familiarize ourselves with a broader range of theoretical traditions than we are accustomed to reading. To do otherwise would be to continue on as we have been: insisting that the individual voter is responsible for the direction of democratic politics; acting as if voting behavior and party practices live in two separate worlds; sidestepping the role of the state; and assuming that our analytical distinctions will bear up under the weight of new data to the contrary. In this, Lipset's impulse to move beyond the Columbia model is understandable (see pp. 22–3, 116–18). What remains is for us to transcend the orthodoxies of both his, and now our own, past.

Notes

Introduction

1 A search of Google Scholar on December 11, 2012, revealed that the foundational works of voter-centered approaches received 28,905 citations, whereas those of party-centered approaches received 10,313. The number of citations for each book is as follows: Lazarsfeld et al.'s *The People's Choice* (4,739), Campbell et al.'s *The American Voter* (5,587), Downs' *An Economic Theory of Democracy* (18,579), Michels' *Political Parties* (3,489), Lipset's *Political Man* (6,107), and Przeworski and Sprague's *Paper Stones* (717). Note that the most widely cited work is Downs. As Carmines and Huckfeldt (1996) write, the Downsian rational choice model has become the dominant voter-centered theory in the literature.

2 Machiavelli and Montesquieu had conceived of parties quite literally as "parts" of the whole polity (e.g., the Nobles and Plebians), but as Sartori (1976: 5–6) makes clear, it was not until the British theorists, and above all Edmund Burke, that party was conceived of as "an *object* term, that is, as a concrete noun that pointed to a concrete entity or agency."

3 I mean this literally, as women were prohibited from voting and running for office.

Chapter 1: The Social Voter

1 An electoral coalition consists of the social groups that a given political party wins a majority of: the Republicans might be said to win a majority of whites, rural voters, affluent voters, native-born voters, and Protestants, whereas the Democrats might be said to carry a majority of urban voters, low- to middle-income voters, immigrant voters, voters of color, as well as Jewish and Catholic voters.

Chapter 2: The Partisan Voter

1 Others, especially Margolis (1977), appear in chapter 3 as a counterpoint to the issue voter approach.

Chapter 3: The Issue Voter

1 Duncan Black's (1958) book, *The Theory of Committees and Elections* is the classic proof of the decisiveness of the median voter in committee voting, though Downs (1957) is credited with proving it for mass elections. Like Downs, Black assumes "peaked preferences" and the dominance of the "median optimum" position. On peaked preferences, he writes, "When a member values the motions before a committee in a definite order, it is reasonable to assume that, when these motions are put against each other, he votes in accordance with his valuation, i.e., in accordance with his schedule of preferences" ([1958] 1963: 5). For example, if the committee member prefers motion 1 (one) the least, 2 (two) the most, and is indifferent to motions 3 (three) and 4 (four), then Black assumes that the committee member will vote for motion 2, vote against motion 1, and abstain from voting on motions 3 and 4. Black refers to the median voter as the "median optimum" position: "If the members' curves are single-peaked," then the median position will be able to get "a simple majority over any other motions . . . put forward" ([1958] 1963: 18).

Chapter 4: The Oligarchical Party

1 This is in fact Lipset's reading of Tocqueville (see, for example, Lipset 1962: 4–9).

2 For a discussion of Weber's distinction of ideological and patronage parties, see chapter 8 of John Levi Martin's (2009) *Social Structures*.

3 Though some have claimed that Weber was somewhat more optimistic about the prospects of democracy than Robert Michels whom we consider next (see, for instance, Roth 1968: lxv), I find that Weber dismisses even charismatic leadership as a promising source of change – this despite the fact that charisma looms large in Weber's work as an alternative to bureaucratic organization. "As a rule," he writes, "the party organization easily succeeds in this castration of charisma" ([1922] 1968: 1132).

4 This is not to say that all political scientists are pluralists. Recently, Hacker and Pierson (2010) and Gilens (2012), among other political scientists, have argued that the wealthy have a disproportionate share of influence on American public policy. Mudge and Chen (2013) point to such works as evidence of a "sociological turn" in political science.

5 In 2010, the U.S. Supreme Court held in *Citizens United* that restrictions on "electioneering communications" 60 days prior to a general election campaign

or 30 days prior to a primary were an abridgment of free speech. The ruling allowed for unlimited campaign advertisements.

6 This, of course, is a highly problematic distinction as we shall see below. For example, some aspects of urban politics in the United States are still based on patronage. The city of Providence, where I live and work, is a notorious example, as is the city of Chicago.

Chapter 5: The Functional Party

1 In this sense, Key, like Lipset, might well be read as bridging the voter- and party-centered divide. Key famously wrote that the term "party" might refer to any number of different groups from the party-in-the-government and the party-in-the-electorate to professional party operatives ([1942] 1964: 163–5). However, the concept of the party-in-the-electorate precedes the concept of individual vote choice by a few years. On my reading, the bridge between voter- and party-centered approaches is clearest in Key's 1961 and 1966 works.

2 Domhoff (1978) would later rebut this claim in *Who Really Rules?* by demonstrating considerable overlap between social and economic notables. See chapter 4 of this book.

3 Lipset's earlier book, *Agrarian Socialism* ([1950] 1967), which is based on the first of his *two* doctoral dissertations at Columbia, is concerned more with Werner Sombart's ([1906] 1976) puzzle, "why is there no socialism in the United States?" than with the conditions enabling democracy. However, an important sub-argument in that book was "a bridge to the study of what would eventually . . . become [his] major substantive and political interest, democracy" (Lipset 1996: 10). As he would later observe of the International Typographical Union, democratic socialism was able to flourish in Saskatchewan in part because of the "high degree of individual participation in community organizations in rural districts. There are from 40,000 to 60,000 different elective rural posts that must be filled by the 125,000 farmers" ([1950] 1967: 200).

4 An interesting counterpoint to Lipset's concern for unchecked division is Samuel P. Huntington's early work on political parties. Huntington argues that political instability in mid-twentieth-century Africa, Asia, and Latin America is due to a "political gap," in which the development of institutions such as parties lags behind the expansion of political consciousness and participation that results from rapid socioeconomic change (1968: 4–5, 397–9). Here Huntington is similar to Lipset in that parties comprise an institutional counterweight to instability. But, whereas Lipset came to view communism as an extremist force, disruptive of order, Huntington compares the Soviet Union favorably with the United States and Great Britain for having developed "strong, adaptable, coherent political institutions." Thus, while it is true that

communists overthrow governments (as Lipset would be quick to point out), they are nevertheless, according to Huntington, "good at making governments ... They may not provide liberty, but they do provide authority; they do create governments that can govern" (1968: 1, 8).

Chapter 6: The Exclusive Party

1 Some justification must be made for not including Carl Schmitt in this chapter ([1932] 1996). Schmitt argued famously that "the concept of the political" was the prerogative to distinguish between "friend and enemy" ([1932] 1996: 26). But for Schmitt, that prerogative belongs primarily to the state, and specifically in its capacity to make war with other states. Thus, parties may be equated with "politics" only in the very limited case of civil war: that is, "if domestic conflicts among political parties have become the sole political difference ... i.e., the domestic, not the foreign friend-and-enemy group-ings are decisive for armed conflict" ([1932] 1996: 32). To name one group a friend and another an enemy is therefore to declare the possibility of war between states or within a state. Schmitt's concept of the political does *not* refer to the symbolic "combat" between political parties, which is an impor-tant point of emphasis in this chapter.
2 Budge and Keman (1990) also suggest that office-seeking is not the only goal of political parties. Their alternative perspective and that of their associates is "policy pursuit."
3 I write that Lenin was critical of economic determinism and not of Kautsky per se, because Lenin's view of the latter shifted over time from approval to disdain.
4 Gramsci's critique of economic determinism was also shaped by the Hegelian anti-positivism of the early twentieth century in both its Marxist (e.g., Labriola) and non-Marxist (e.g., Croce, Sorel) forms.
5 Przeworski would later abandon the Marxist framework in favor of rational choice theory. For example, in theorizing the prospects for economic reform in Eastern Europe and Latin America, he explicitly states that "socialism ... is not feasible because it rests on untenable assumptions concerning the behavior of planners, of workers, and of consumers." Though he remains critical of the intrinsic irrationality of capitalism, he also argues, on the basis of a rational actor model that with respect to political reform, "democracies last when they evoke self-interested compliance from the major political forces" (1991: x–xi).
6 There are also several non-Marxist critiques of moderation theory (see Kalyvas 1996, Schwedler 2006, and Tezcür 2010). Schwedler, for instance, finds that whereas the Islamic Action Front in Jordan became more moder-ate with participation in the political process, the Islah Party of Yemen did not. There are several factors that explain this variation, but, she writes, the decisive one was that "reconciling a broader Islamist agenda with democratic

practices was less crucial to the Islah party than it had been for Jordan's IAF" (2006: 197).

7 Another stream within Marxism, vaguely represented here by Althusser but better articulated elsewhere by Poulantzas (1969) and Miliband (1970), is that the capitalist state is "relatively autonomous" of class forces: it is not exactly the executive committee of the bourgeoisie as Marx and Engels once wrote ([1848] 1998: 37), but it is institutionally predisposed to serve bourgeois interests.

References

Abrams, Philip. 1988. "Notes on the Difficulty of Studying the State." *Journal of Historical Sociology* 1: 58–89.

Abramson, Paul R., John H. Aldrich, and David W. Rohde. 2010. *Continuity and Change in the 2008 Elections*. Washington, DC: Congressional Quarterly Press.

Aldrich, John H. 1995. *Why Parties? The Origin and Transformation of Political Parties in America*. Chicago, IL: University of Chicago Press.

Aldrich, John H. 2005. "The Election of 1800: The Consequences of the First Change in Party Control." Pp. 23–38 in *Establishing Congress: the removal to Washington, D.C. and the election of 1800*, edited by Kenneth R. Bowling and Donald R. Kennon. Athens, OH: Ohio University Press.

Althusser, Louis. [1970] 2001. "Ideology and Ideological State Apparatuses." Pp. 127–86 in *Lenin and Philosophy and Other Essays*, translated from the French by Ben Brewster. New York: Monthly Review Press.

Alvarez, R. Michael and Jonathan Nagler. 2004. "Party System Compactness: Measurement and Consequences." *Political Analysis* 12: 46–62.

American Political Science Association. 1950. "Toward a More Responsible Two-Party System." *American Political Science Review* 44 (3), Part 2, Supplement: v–96.

Aminzade, Ronald. 1993. *Ballots and Barricades: Class Formation and Republican Politics in France, 1830–1871*. Princeton, NJ: Princeton University Press.

Auyero, Javier. 2001. *Poor People's Politics: Peronist Survival Networks and the Legacy of Evita*. Durham, NC: Duke University Press.

Azani, Eitan. 2009. *Hezbollah: The Story of the Party of God: from Revolution to Institutionalization*. New York: Palgrave Macmillan.

Bachrach, Peter. 1967. *The Theory of Democratic Elitism: a Critique*. Boston: Little, Brown and Company.

Baldassarri, Delia and Andrew Gelman. 2008. "Partisans without Constraint:

References

Political Polarization and Trends in American Public Opinion." *American Journal of Sociology* 114 (2): 408–46.

Banfield, Edward C. and James Q. Wilson. 1967. *City Politics*. Cambridge, MA: Harvard University Press.

Beck, Paul Allen. 1974. "A Socialization Theory of Partisan Realignment." Pp. 199–219 in *The Politics of Future Citizens: New Dimensions in the Political Socialization of Children*. San Francisco, CA: Jossey-Bass.

Berelson, Bernard, Paul F. Lazarsfeld, and William McPhee. 1954. *Voting: A Study of Opinion Formation in a Presidential Campaign*. Chicago, IL: University of Chicago Press.

Black, Duncan. [1958] 1963. *The Theory of Committees and Elections*. Cambridge: Cambridge University Press.

Bolingbroke, Henry St. John. [1749] 1965. *The Idea of a Patriot King*. Indianapolis, IN: Bobbs-Merrill.

Brady, David W. 1988. *Critical Elections and Congressional Policy Making*. Stanford, CA: Stanford University Press.

Brewer, Mark D. and Jeffrey M. Stonecash. 2007. *Split: Class and Cultural Divides in American Politics*. Washington, DC: CQ Press.

Bridges, Amy. [1984] 1987. *A City in the Republic: Antebellum New York and the Origins of Machine Politics*. Ithaca, NY: Cornell University Press

Budge, Ian and Hans Keman. 1990. *Parties and Democracy: Coalition Formation and Government Functioning in Twenty States*. Oxford: Oxford University Press.

Burawoy, Michael. 1989. "Marxism without Micro-Foundations." *Socialist Review* 89 (2): 53–86.

Burke, Edmund. 1770. *Thoughts on the Cause of the Present Discontents*. Dublin and London: J. Dodsley.

Burnham, Walter Dean. 1970. *Critical Elections and the Mainsprings of American Politics*. New York: Norton.

Burstein, Paul. 1998. "Interest Organizations, Political Parties, and the Study of Democratic Politics." Pp. 39–56 in *Social Movements and American Political Institutions*, edited by Anne N. Costain and Andrew S. McFarland. Lanham, MD: Rowman & Littlefield.

Butler, David and Donald Stokes. [1969] 1974. *Political Change in Britain: The Evolution of Electoral Choice* (Second Edition). New York: St. Martin's Press.

Buxton, William. 1985. *Talcott Parsons and the Capitalist Nation-State: Political Sociology as a Strategic Vocation*. Toronto: University of Toronto Press.

Campbell, Angus, Gerald Gurin, and Warren E. Miller. 1954. *The Voter Decides*. Evanston, IL and White Plains, NY: Row, Peterson and Company.

Campbell, Angus, Philip E. Converse, Warren E. Miller, and Donald E. Stokes. 1960. *The American Voter*. New York: John Wiley & Sons.

Carmines, Edward G. and Robert Huckfeldt. 1996. "Political Behavior: An Overview." Pp. 223–54 in *A New Handbook of Political Science*, edited by

References

Robert E. Goodin and Hans-Dieter Klingemann. Oxford: Oxford University Press.

Carmines, Edward G. and James A. Stimson. 1989. *Issue Evolution: Race and the Transformation of American Politics.* Princeton, NJ: Princeton University Press.

Carmines, Edward G., John P. McIver, and James A. Stimson. 1987. "Unrealized Partisanship: A Theory of Dealignment." *Journal of Politics* 49 (2): 376–400.

Census of India. 2011. "Distribution of Population by Religions." *Drop-in-Article on Census* 4: 1–5. http://censusindia.gov.in/Ad_Campaign/drop_in_articles/04-Distribution_by_Religion.pdf (accessed Dec. 12, 2012).

Clawson, Dan, Alan Neustadtl, and Denise Scott. 1992. *Money Talks: Corporate PACs and Political Influence.* New York: Basic Books.

Clubb, Jerome M., William H. Flannigan, and Nancy H. Zingale. 1980. *Partisan Realignment: Voters, Parties, and Government in American History.* Beverly Hills, CA: Sage.

Cohen, Jean and Andrew Arato. 1992. *Civil Society and Political Theory.* Cambridge, MA: MIT Press.

Converse, Philip E. 1964. "The Nature of Belief Systems in Mass Publics." Pp. 206–261 in *Ideology and Discontent,* edited by David E. Apter. Glencoe, IL: Free Press and London: Collier Macmillan.

Converse, Philip E. 1966. "The Concept of a Normal Vote." Pp. 9–39 in *Elections and the Political Order,* edited by Angus Campbell, Philip E. Converse, Warren E. Miller, and Donald A. Stokes. New York: Wiley.

Converse, Philip E. 2006. "Researching Electoral Politics." *American Political Science Review* 100 (4): 605–12.

Dahl, Robert A. 1961. *Who Governs? Democracy and Power in an American City.* New Haven, CT: Yale University Press.

Davis, Otto A. and Melvin J. Hinich. 1966. "Some results related to a mathematical model of policy formation in a democratic society." Carnegie Institute of Technology, Graduate School of Industrial Administration.

de Leon, Cedric. 2008. "'No Bourgeois Mass Party, No Democracy': The Missing Link in Barrington Moore's American Civil War." *Political Power and Social Theory* 19: 39–82.

de Leon, Cedric. 2010. "Vicarious Revolutionaries: Martial Discourse and the Origins of Mass Party Competition in the United States, 1789–1848." *Studies in American Political Development* 24: 121–41.

de Leon, Cedric, Manali Desai, and Cihan Tuğal. 2009. "Political Articulation: Parties and the Constitution of Cleavages in the United States, India, and Turkey." *Sociological Theory* 27 (3): 193–219.

DiMaggio, Paul, John Evans, and Bethany Bryson. 1996. "Have Americans' Social Attitudes Become More Polarized?" *American Journal of Sociology* 102 (3): 690–755.

References

Dodd, Lawrence C. 1976. *Coalitions in Parliamentary Government*. Princeton, NJ: Princeton University Press.

Domhoff, G. William. 1978. *Who Really Rules? New Haven and Community Power Reexamined*. Santa Monica, CA: Goodyear Publishing Company.

Domhoff, G. William. 1998. *Who Rules America? Power and Politics in the Year 2000* (Third Edition). Mountain View, CA: Mayfield Publishing Company.

Downs, Anthony. 1957. *An Economic Theory of Democracy*. New York: Harper & Row.

Duverger, Maurice. [1951] 1963. *Political Parties: Their Organization and Activity in the Modern State*. New York: John Wiley & Sons.

Edelman, Murray. [1964] 1974. *The Symbolic Uses of Politics*. Urbana, IL: University of Illinois Press.

Enelow, James M. and Melvin J. Hinich. 1982. "Ideology, Issues, and the Spatial Theory of Elections." *American Political Science Review* 76: 493–501.

Enelow, James M. and Melvin J. Hinich. 1984. *The Spatial Theory of Voting: An Introduction*. Cambridge: Cambridge University Press.

Ferling, John. 2004. *Adams vs. Jefferson: the Tumultuous Election of 1800*. New York: Oxford University Press.

Fiorina, Morris P. 1981. *Retrospective Voting in American National Elections*. New Haven, CT: Yale University Press.

Fiorina, Morris with Samuel J. Abrams and Jeremy C. Pope. 2005. *Culture War? The Myth of a Polarized America*. New York: Pearson Longman.

Frank, Thomas. 2004. *What's the Matter with Kansas? How Conservatives Won the Heart of America*. New York: Metropolitan Books.

Franklin, Mark N. 1985. *The Decline of Class Voting in Britain: Changes in the Basis of Electoral Choice, 1964–1983*. Oxford: Clarendon Press.

Fraser, Steve and Gary Gerstle (eds). 1989. *The Rise and Fall of the New Deal Order, 1930–1980*. Princeton, NJ: Princeton University Press.

Gerteis, Joseph. 2003. "Populism, race, and political interest in Virginia." *Social Science History* 27: 197–227.

Gerteis, Joseph. 2007. *Class and the Color Line: Interracial Class Coalition in the Knights of Labor and the Populist Movement*. Durham, NC: Duke University Press.

Gilens, Martin. 2012. *Affluence and Influence: Economic Inequality and Political Power in America*. New York: Russell Sage Foundation; Princeton, NJ: Princeton University Press.

Glenn, John K. 2003. "Parties out of Movements: Party Emergence in Postcommunist Eastern Europe." Pp. 147–169 in *States, Parties, and Social Movements*, edited by Jack A. Goldstone. Cambridge: Cambridge University Press.

Goldstone, Jack A. (ed.). 2003. *States, Parties, and Social Movements*. Cambridge: Cambridge University Press.

Gramsci, Antonio. [1921] 2000. "Parties and Masses." Pp. 121–5 in *The Antonio*

References

Gramsci Reader, Selected Writings 1916–1935, edited by David Forgacs. New York: New York University Press.

Gramsci, Antonio. [1926] 1992. "The Southern Question." Pp. 28–51 in *The Modern Prince & Other Writings*, by Antonio Gramsci. New York: International Publishers.

Gramsci, Antonio. 1971. *Selections from the Prison Notebooks*, edited and translated by Quintin Hoare and Geoffrey Nowell Smith. New York: International Publishers.

Green, Donald, Bradley Palmquist, and Eric Schickler. 2002. *Partisan Hearts and Minds: Political Parties and the Social Identities of Voters*. New Haven, CT: Yale University Press.

Gunning, Jeroen. 2008. *Hamas in Politics: Democracy, Religion, Violence*. New York: Columbia University Press.

Habermas, Jurgen. 1991. *The Structural Transformation of the Public Sphere: an Inquiry into a Category of Bourgeois Society*. Cambridge, MA: MIT Press.

Hacker, Jacob S. and Paul Pierson. 2010. *Winner-Take-All Politics: How Washington Made the Rich Richer – And Turned Its Back on the Middle Class*. New York: Simon and Schuster.

Hofstadter, Richard. 1969. *The Idea of a Party System: The Rise of Legitimate Opposition in the United States, 1780–1840*. Berkeley, CA: University of California Press.

Hotelling, Harold. 1929. "Stability in Competition." *The Economic Journal* 39: 41–57.

Hroub, Khaled. 2010. *Hamas: a Beginner's Guide* (Second Edition). New York: Pluto Press.

Hume, David. [1758] 1854. "Of the Coalition of Parties." Pp. 523–32 in *The Philosophical Works of David Hume*. Boston: Little, Brown and Company; Edinburgh: Adam and Charles Black.

Hunter, Floyd. [1953] 1963. *Community Power Structure: A Study of Decision Makers*. New York: Anchor.

Huntington, Samuel P. 1968. *Political Order in Changing Societies*. New Haven, CT: Yale University Press.

Inglehart, Ronald. 1990. *Culture Shift in Advanced Industrial Society*. Princeton, NJ: Princeton University Press.

Iversen, Torben. 1994. "Political Leadership and Representation in West European Democracies: A Test of Three Models of Voting." *American Journal of Political Science* 38 (1): 45–74.

Jaber, Hala. 1997. *Hezbollah: Born with a Vengeance*. New York: Columbia University Press.

Jessop, Bob. 1990. *State Theory: Putting the Capitalist State in its Place*. Cambridge: Polity.

Kalyvas, Stathis N. 1996. *The Rise of Christian Democracy in Europe*. Ithaca, NY: Cornell University Press.

References

Katz, Richard S. and Peter Mair. 1995. "Changing Models of Party Organization and Party Democracy: The Emergence of the Cartel Party." *Party Politics* 1 (1): 5–28.

Katz, Richard S. and Peter Mair. 2009. "The Cartel Party Thesis: A Restatement." *Perspectives on Politics* 7 (4): 753–66.

Kautsky, Karl. 1910. *The Class Struggle.* Chicago, IL: C.H. Kerr and Co.

Key, V.O., Jr. [1942] 1964. *Politics, Parties, & Pressure Groups* (Fifth Edition). New York: Thomas Y. Crowell Company.

Key, V.O. 1954. "Foreword." Pp. ix–xiii in *The Voter Decides*, by Angus Campbell, Gerald Gurin, and Warren E. Miller. Evanston, IL and White Plains, NY: Row, Peterson and Company.

Key, V.O., Jr. 1955. "A Theory of Critical Elections." *Journal of Politics* 17: 3–18.

Key, V.O., Jr. 1959. "Secular Realignment and the Party System." *Journal of Politics* 21: 198–210.

Key, V.O., Jr. [1961] 1964. *Public Opinion and American Democracy.* New York: Knopf.

Key, V.O., Jr. 1966. *The Responsible Electorate: Rationality in Presidential Voting, 1936–1960.* Cambridge, MA: Belknap Press of Harvard University Press.

Key, V.O., Jr. and Frank Munger. 1959. "Social Determinism and Electoral Decision: the Case of Indiana." Pp. 281–299 in *American Voting Behavior*, edited by Eugene Burdick and Arthur J. Brodbeck. New York: Free Press; London: Collier-Macmillan.

Kinder, Donald R. and D. Roderick Kiewiet. 1981. "Sociotropic Politics: The American Case." *British Journal of Political Science* 11 (2): 129–61.

Kitschelt, Herbert and Steven I. Wilkinson. 2007. "Citizen-politician linkages: an introduction." Pp. 1–49 in *Patrons, Clients, and Policies: Patterns of Democratic Accountability and Political Competition*, edited by Herbert Kitschelt and Steven I. Wilkinson. Cambridge: Cambridge University Press.

Knoke, David. 1976. *Change and Continuity in American Politics: The Social Bases of Political Parties.* Baltimore, MD: The Johns Hopkins University Press.

Laclau, Ernesto and Chantal Mouffe. [1985] 2001. *Hegemony and Socialist Strategy: Towards a Radical Democratic Politics* (Second Edition). New York: Verso.

Lazarsfeld, Paul F., Bernard Berelson, and Hazel Gaudet. [1944] 1948. *The People's Choice: How the Voter Makes Up His Mind in a Presidential Campaign* (Second Edition). New York: Columbia University Press.

Lenin, Vladimir I. [1902] 1973. *What is to be Done?* Peking: Foreign Languages Press.

Leonard, Gerald. 2002. *The Invention of Party Politics: Federalism, Popular Sovereignty, and Constitutional Development in Jacksonian Illinois.* Chapel Hill, NC: University of North Carolina Press.

References

Lipset, Seymour Martin. [1950] 1967. *Agrarian Socialism: The Cooperative Commonwealth Federation in Saskatchewan, A Study in Political Sociology.* Berkeley, CA: University of California Press.

Lipset, Seymour Martin. [1959] 1965. "Political Sociology." Pp. 81–114 in *Sociology Today*, Vol. I, edited by Robert K. Merton, Leonard Broom, and Leonard S. Cottrell, Jr. New York: Basic Books.

Lipset, Seymour Martin. 1960. *Political Man: the Social Bases of Politics.* Garden City, NY: Doubleday.

Lipset, Seymour Martin. 1962. "Introduction." Pp. 15–39 in *Political Parties: A Sociological Study of the Oligarchical Tendencies of Modern Democracy*, by Robert Michels. New York: Free Press; London: Collier-Macmillan.

Lipset, Seymour Martin. 1964. "Introduction: Ostrogorski and the Analytic Approach to the Comparative Study of Political Parties." Pp. ix–lxviii in *Democracy and the Organization of Political Parties, Volume II: The United States*, by Moisei Ostrogorski. Chicago, IL: Quadrangle Books.

Lipset, Seymour Martin. 1988. "This Week's Citation Classic." *Current Contents* no. 20 (May 16): 16. http://garfield.library.upenn.edu/classics1988/A1988N211900001.pdf (accessed Dec. 12, 2012).

Lipset, Seymour Martin. 1996. "Steady Work." *Annual Review of Sociology* 22: 1–27.

Lipset, Seymour Martin and Stein Rokkan. 1967. *Party Systems and Voter Alignments: Cross-National Perspectives.* New York: Free Press.

Lipset, Seymour Martin, Paul F. Lazarsfeld, Allen H. Barton, and Juan Linz. 1954. "The Psychology of Voting: An Analysis of Political Behavior." Pp. 1124–75 in *Handbook of Social Psychology, Volume II, Special Fields and Applications*, edited by Gardner Lindzey. Reading, MA: Addison-Wesley.

Lipset, Seymour Martin, Martin A. Trow, and James S. Coleman. 1956. *Union Democracy: The Internal Politics of the International Typographical Union.* New York: Free Press.

Livingstone, Arthur. 1939. "Introduction." Pp. ix–xxxvi in *The Ruling Class (Elementi di Scienza Politica)*, by Gaetano Mosca. New York: McGraw-Hill.

Lodge, Milton and Patrick Stroh. 1993. "Inside the Mental Voting Booth: An Impression-Driven Process Model of Candidate Evaluation." Pp. 225–63 in *Explorations in Political Psychology*, edited by Shanto Iyengar and William J. McGuire. Durham, NC: Duke University Press.

Manza, Jeff and Clem Brooks. 1999. *Social Cleavages and Political Change: Voter Alignments and U.S. Party Coalitions.* Oxford: Oxford University Press.

Marais, Hein. 2011. *South Africa: Pushed to the Limit: the Political Economy of Change.* New York: Zed Books.

Margolis, Michael. 1977. "From Confusion to Confusion: Issues and the American Voter (1956–1972). *American Political Science Review* 71 (1): 31–43.

References

Martin, John Levi. 2009. *Social Structures*. Princeton, NJ: Princeton University Press.

Marx, Karl. [1852] 1992. "The Eighteenth Brumaire of Louis Bonaparte." Pp. 143–249 in *Surveys from Exile: Political Writings* (Volume 2). London: Penguin Books.

Marx, Karl. [1859] 1978. "Preface to *A Contribution to the Critique of Political Economy*." Pp. 3–6 in *The Marx-Engels Reader* (Second Edition), edited by Robert C. Tucker. New York: Norton.

Marx, Karl and Frederick Engels. [1848] 1998. *The Communist Manifesto: A Modern Edition*. London and New York: Verso.

Mayhew, David R. 2000. "Electoral Realignments." *Annual Review of Political Science* 3: 449–74.

McAdam, Doug and Sidney Tarrow. 2010. "Ballots and Barricades: On the Reciprocal Relationship between Elections and Social Movements." *Perspectives on Politics* 8 (2): 529–42.

McAdam, Doug, Sidney Tarrow, and Charles Tilly. 2001. *Dynamics of Contention*. Cambridge: Cambridge University Press.

McAllister, Ian and Richard Rose. 1986. *Voters Begin to Choose: From Closed-Class to Open Elections in Britain*. London: Sage.

Merrill, Samuel and Bernard Grofman. 1999. *A Unified Theory of Voting: Directional and Proximity Spatial Models*. Cambridge: Cambridge University Press.

Michels, Robert. [1911] 1962. *Political Parties: a Sociological Study of the Oligarchical Tendencies of Modern Democracy*. New York: Free Press.

Miliband, Ralph. 1970. "The Capitalist State: Reply to Nicos Poulantzas." *New Left Review* 58: 53–60.

Miller, Warren E. and J. Merrill Shanks. 1996. *The New American Voter*. Cambridge, MA: Harvard University Press.

Mills, C. Wright. [1956] 1957. *The Power Elite*. New York: Oxford University Press.

Mitchell, Timothy. 1999. "Society, Economy, and the State Effect." Pp. 76–97 in *State/Culture: State-Formation after the Cultural Turn*, edited by George Steinmetz. Ithaca, NY: Cornell University Press.

Mizruchi, Mark S. 1992. *The Structure of Corporate Political Action: Interfirm Relations and Their Consequences*. Cambridge, MA: Harvard University Press.

Mosca, Gaetano. [1896] 1939. *The Ruling Class (Elementi di Scienza Politica)*. New York: McGraw-Hill.

Mudge, Stephanie L. and Anthony S. Chen. 2013. "Political Parties in the Sociological Imagination: Past, Present, and Future Directions." *Annual Review of Sociology* 39 (forthcoming).

Nie, Norman H., Sidney Verba, and John R. Petrocik. [1976] 1979. *The Changing American Voter* (enlarged edition). Cambridge, MA: Harvard University Press.

References

Ostrogorski, Moisei. [1902] 1964. *Democracy and the Organization of Political Parties, Volume II: The United States*. Chicago, IL: Quadrangle Books.

Pareto, Vilfredo. [1901] 1968. *The Rise and Fall of the Elites: An Application of Theoretical Sociology*. Totowa, NJ: Bedminster Press.

Parsons, Talcott. 1951. *The Social System*. Glencoe, IL: Free Press.

Pierson, Paul. 2004. *Politics in Time: History, Institutions, and Social Analysis*. Princeton, NJ: Princeton University Press.

Polsby, Nelson W. 1963. *Community Power and Political Theory*. New Haven, CT: Yale University Press.

Pomper, Gerald M. 1972. "From Confusion to Clarity: Issues and American Voters, 1956–1968." *American Political Science Review* 66: 415–28.

Poole, Keith T. and Howard Rosenthal. 1997. *Congress: A Political-Economic History of Roll Call Voting*. Oxford: Oxford University Press.

Popkin, Samuel L. 1991. *The Reasoning Voter: Communication and Persuasion in Presidential Campaigns*. Chicago, IL: University of Chicago Press.

Poulantzas, Nicos. 1969. "The Problem of the Capitalist State." *New Left Review* 58: 67–78.

Przeworski, Adam. 1977. "Proletariat into a Class: The Process of Class Formation from Karl Kautsky's *The Class Struggle* to Recent Controversies." *Politics and Society* 7: 343–401.

Przeworski, Adam. 1991. *Democracy and the Market: Political and Economic Reforms in Eastern Europe and Latin America*. Cambridge: Cambridge University Press.

Przeworski, Adam and John Sprague. 1986. *Paper Stones: A History of Electoral Socialism*. Chicago, IL: University of Chicago Press.

Pugh, Jeff. 2008. "Vectors of Contestation: Social Movements and Party Systems in Ecuador and Colombia." *Latin American Essays* XXI: 1–18.

Rabinowitz, George and Stuart Macdonald. 1989. "A Directional Theory of Issue Voting." *American Political Science Review* 83 (1): 93–121.

Rahn, Wendy M., John H. Aldrich, Eugene Borgida, and John L. Sullivan. 1990. "A Social Cognitive Model of Candidate Appraisal." Pp. 136–59 in *Information and Democratic Processes*, edited by John A. Ferejohn and James H. Kuklinski. Urbana, IL: University of Illinois Press.

Redding, Kent. 2003. *Making Race, Making Power: North Carolina's Road to Disfranchisement*. Urbana, IL: University of Illinois Press.

Rieder, Jonathan. 1989. "The Rise of the 'Silent Majority.'" Pp. 243–68 in *The Rise and Fall of the New Deal Order, 1930–1980*, edited by Steve Fraser and Gary Gerstle. Princeton, NJ: Princeton University Press.

Riker, William H. 1962. *The Theory of Political Coalitions*. New Haven, CT: Yale University Press.

Riley, Dylan and Manali Desai. 2007. "The Passive Revolutionary Route to the Modern World: Italy and India in Comparative Perspective." *Comparative Studies in Society and History* 49 (4): 815–47.

References

Robbins, Caroline. 1958. "'Discordant Parties': A Study of the Acceptance of Party by Englishmen." *Political Science Quarterly* 73 (4): 505–29.

Rossi, Peter H. 1959. "Four Landmarks in Voting Research." Pp. 5–54 in *American Voting Behavior*, edited by Eugene Burdick and Arthur J. Brodbeck. New York: Free Press; London: Collier-Macmillan.

Rossiter, Clinton. 1960. *Parties and Politics in America*. Ithaca, NY: Cornell University Press.

Roth, Guenther. 1968. "Introduction." Pp xxxiii–cx in *Economy and Society: An Outline of Interpretive Sociology*, edited by Guenther Roth and Claus Wittich. New York: Bedminster Press.

Roy, Sara. 2011. *Hamas and Civil Society in Gaza: Engaging the Islamist Social Sector*. Princeton, NJ: Princeton University Press.

Sartori, Giovanni. 1969. "From the Sociology of Politics to Political Sociology." Pp. 65–100 in *Politics and the Social Sciences*, edited by Seymour Martin Lipset. New York: Oxford University Press.

Sartori, Giovanni. 1976. *Parties and Party Systems: A Framework for Analysis, Volume I*. Cambridge: Cambridge University Press.

Schattschneider, E.E. [1942] 1967. *Party Government*. New York: Holt, Rinehart and Winston.

Schattschneider, E.E. [1960] 1983. *The Semisovereign People: a Realist's View of Democracy in America*. New York: Holt, Rinehart and Winston.

Schier, Steven E. 2000. *By Invitation Only: The Rise of Exclusive Politics in the United States*. Pittsburgh, PA: University of Pittsburgh Press.

Schmitt, Carl. [1932] 1996. *The Concept of the Political*. Chicago, IL: University of Chicago Press.

Schumpeter, Joseph A. [1942] 1975. *Capitalism, Socialism and Democracy* (Third Edition). New York: Harper Colophon Books.

Schwartz, Mildred A. 2006. *Party Movements in the United States and Canada: Strategies and Persistence*. Lanham, MD: Rowman and Littlefield.

Schwedler, Jillian. 2006. *Faith in Moderation: Islamist Parties in Jordan and Yemen*. Cambridge: Cambridge University Press.

Scott, James C. 1972. *Comparative Political Corruption*. Englewood Cliffs, NJ: Prentice-Hall.

Sears, David O., Carl P. Hensler, and Leslie K. Speer. 1979. "Whites' Opposition to 'Busing': Self-Interest or Symbolic Politics." *American Political Science Review* 73 (2): 369–84.

Shefter, Martin. [1977] 1994. *Political Parties and the State: The American Historical Experience*. Princeton, NJ: Princeton University Press.

Slez, Adam and John Levi Martin. 2007. "Political Action and Party Formation in the United States Constitutional Convention." *American Sociological Review* 72 (1): 42–67.

Smith, Eric R.A.N. 1989. *The Unchanging American Voter*. Berkeley, CA: University of California Press.

References

Smithies, Arthur. 1941. "Optimum Location in Spatial Competition." *Journal of Political Economy* 49: 423–39.

Sombart, Werner. [1906] 1976. *Why is there no Socialism in the United States?* White Plains, NY: International Arts and Sciences Press.

Sorel, Georges. [1908] 1969. *The Illusions of Progress*. Berkeley, CA: University of California Press.

Stokes, Donald E. 1963. "Spatial Models of Party Competition." *American Political Science Review* 57 (2): 368–77.

Sundquist, James L. 1983. *Dynamics of the Party System: Alignment and Realignment of Political Parties in the United States*. Washington, DC: The Brookings Institution.

Tezcür, Gunes Mürat. 2010. *Muslim Reformers in Iran and Turkey: The Paradox of Moderation*. Austin, TX: University of Texas Press.

Tocqueville, Alexis de. [1835] 1965. *Democracy in America*, Volume I, translated by Henry Reeve. New Rochelle, NY: Arlington House.

Tucker, Robert C. (ed.) 1978. *The Marx-Engels Reader* (Second Edition). New York: Norton.

Tuğal, Cihan. 2009. *Passive Revolution: Absorbing the Islamic Challenge to Capitalism*. Stanford, CA: Stanford University Press.

Valelly, Richard M. 2004. *The Two Reconstructions: the Struggle for Black Enfranchisement*. Chicago, IL: University of Chicago Press.

Van Buren, Martin. 1973. *The Autobiography of Martin Van Buren*, Volume II. New York: Da Capo Press.

Van Engeland, Anisseh. 2008a. "Hezbollah: from a Terrorist Group to a Political Party – Social Work as a Key to Politics." Pp. 29–49 in *From Terrorism to Politics*, edited by Anisseh Van Engeland and Rachael M. Rudolph. Burlington, VT: Ashgate.

Van Engeland, Anisseh. 2008b. "A Successful 'Turn Over': the African National Congress Moves from Sabotage to a Legitimate Political Force and from Apartheid to Democracy." Pp. 13–27 in *From Terrorism to Politics*, edited by Anisseh Van Engeland and Rachael M. Rudolph. Burlington, VT: Ashgate.

Von Neumann, John and Oskar Morgenstern. 1944. *The Theory of Games and Economic Behavior*. Princeton, NJ: Princeton University Press.

Walker, Jack L. 1966. "A Critique of the Elitist Theory of Democracy." *American Political Science Review* 60 (2): 285–95.

Washington, George. [1796] 1904. "Farewell Address." Pp. 213–24 in *A Compilation of the Messages and Papers of the Presidents, 1789–1902*, Volume I, edited by James D. Richardson and the Joint Committee on Printing, United States Senate. Washington, DC: Bureau of National Literature and Art.

Wattenberg, Ben J. 1995. *Values Matter Most: How Republicans or Democrats or a Third Party Can Win and Renew the American Way of Life*. New York: Free Press.

Weber, Max. [1922] 1968. *Economy and Society: An Outline of Interpretive*

Sociology, edited by Guenther Roth and Claus Wittich. New York: Bedminster Press.

Weber, Max. 1946. *From Max Weber: Essays in Sociology*, edited by H.H. Gerth and C. Wright Mills. New York: Oxford University Press.

Westen, Drew. 2007. *The Political Brain: The Role of Emotion in Deciding the Fate of the Nation*. New York: Public Affairs.

White, John Kenneth. 2006. "What is a Political Party?" Pp. 5–15 in *Handbook of Party Politics*, edited by Richard S. Katz and William Crotty. London: Sage.

Wilentz, Sean. 2005. *The Rise of American Democracy: Jefferson to Lincoln*. New York: Norton.

Wilson, Major. 1988. "Republicanism and the Idea of Party in the Jacksonian Period. *Journal of the Early Republic* 8 (4): 419–42.

Wilson, Woodrow. 1905. *Constitutional Government in the United States*. New York: Columbia University Press.

Yashar, Deborah J. 2005. *Contesting Citizenship in Latin America: The Rise of Indigenous Movements and the Postliberal Challenge*. New York: Cambridge University Press.

Zald, Mayer N. and Michael A. Berger. 1978. "Social Movements in Organizations: Coup de'État, Insurgency, and Mass Movements." *American Journal of Sociology* 83 (4): 823–61.

Zaller, John R. 1992. *The Nature and Origins of Mass Opinion*. Cambridge: Cambridge University Press.

Zetterberg, Hans L. 1968. "Introduction: Pareto's Theory of the Elites." Pp. 1–22 in *The Rise and Fall of the Elites: An Application of Theoretical Sociology*, by Vilfredo Pareto. Totowa, NJ: Bedminster Press.

Index

Index

Index

Index

Index

Index

Index

Index

Van Buren, Martin 9–10
Vietnam 11
Vietnam War
  issue voters 42, 57, 63, 72
  values voters 25
voluntary groups 1
Von Neumann, John
  N-person games 125–6
The Voter Decides (Campbell et al.)
  35–6
voters
  exclusive parties and 146
  functional parties and 106,
   108
  microtargeting of 160–1
  oligarchical parties and 5, 78, 82,
   84, 86, 94, 96, 97, 99
  sociological interest in 4
voters, issue
  comparison to partisan 57
  directional theory 49–51
  ideological immobility of 59
  median voter 60–1
  multidimensional model 65–6
  origins of 57–8
  peaked preferences 38, 59,
   168n1
  pocketbook politics 67
  realignment theory 63–4
  retrospective voting 66–7
  reward-punishment thesis 66
  sociotropic voting 67
  spatial theory 58–61
voters, partisan 4–5
  constraint 40, 45
  directional theory 49–51
  exclusive party and 160–1
  family and 32, 37
  funnel of causality 36, 43
  irrationality of 49, 154
  loyalty to political group
   33–4
  party ID 32, 36, 37, 41, 43–4
  polarization debates 44–6
  schema theory 47–55
  social psychological/Michigan
   model 35–42

spatial theory and 38–40
voters, social 12
  Columbia model of 19–22,
   117–18
  cultural values 24–6
  neoclassical theories of 26–9
  partisan *versus* 4–5
Voting (Berelson, Lazarsfeld and
  McPhee) 21, 30, 120

War on Terror 2
Washington, George
  Farewell Address 8–9
  Whiskey Rebellion 9
Wattenberg, Ben 26
Weber, Max 5
  bureaucracy 84–5
  ideal type 41
  Iron Rule 75
  notion of state 1, 162
  one-party states 83–4
  Ostrogorski's influence on
   76
  Tocqueville's influence on
   76
welfare state 24–6, 108, 155
  omnibus parties as 158
Westen, Drew
  The Political Brain 54–5
What is to be Done? (Lenin) 141,
  148
What's the Matter with Kansas?
  (Frank) 29
Whigs
  versus Court 6
  'Whig Theory' 105
Whiskey Rebellion 9
Who Governs? (Dahl) 114–15
Who Really Rules? (Domhoff)
  90–1
Wilkinson, Steven I. 96–7
Willkie, Wendell 20
Wilson, James Q. 96
  City Politics (with Banfield) 93–5
Wilson, Woodrow
  *Constitutional Government in the
  United States* 104–5